UNCOMMON
HOPE

THE PATH TO AN
EPIC LIFE

KURT W. BUBNA

"As a purpose-driven pastor, Kurt W. Bubna provides encouraging insight into discovering an epic life of uncommon hope."

—Pastor Rick Warren, senior pastor of Saddleback Church, author of *The Purpose Driven Church* and *The Purpose Driven Life*

"Author Kurt W. Bubna unlocks the secret to an epic life. Spoiler alert, it is hope, uncommon hope. In true Bubna fashion, Kurt speaks to his reader as if he is hanging out with a good buddy. His style is relatable, raw, humorous, humble, and practical. You won't be smacked with platitudes but instead will have a friend who sits beside you and encourages you. Kurt masterfully equips his readers to meet struggles head-on and embrace hope. If you are struggling with a relationship, poor personal choices, or a loss, this book is for you."

—Lori Wildenberg, speaker and author of five books, including *Messy Journey: How Grace and Truth Offer the Prodigal a Way Home*

"We all struggle with challenges that threaten to leave us hopeless. Bubna offers an inspiring path to hope that will lead you back to God's amazing plan for your life! I highly recommend this encouraging book."

—Chris Norton, speaker, author of *The Seven Longest Yards*

"Kurt W. Bubna is a prisoner of hope. He wields stories to attack our doubts and pull us back from the brink of despair. He uses Scripture to deftly inject grace and love into our guilt and self-hatred."

—Jim Henderson, author of *Jim and Casper Go to Church*

"Kurt W. Bubna is the real deal. His writing style makes you feel as if you're sitting with him having a cup of coffee discussing real life and how God intersects our everyday issues in extraordinary ways. Kurt is sharing as a fellow sojourner in this sometimes confusing maze we call life. He shares stories you can relate to along with truths you needed to remember. If you need to hear more about the God who walks with you through everything life throws at you, *Uncommon Hope* is for you!"

—Dr. Brian Moss, lead pastor of
Oak Ridge Baptist Church, Salisbury, Maryland

"Do you like reading about yourself? Seeing your story in print? If so, read Kurt W. Bubna's new book, *Uncommon Hope*. If not, give it to a friend. I promise that you'll identify with Kurt's stories of struggle and hope—they will resonate because they are universal. This is us. But Kurt gracefully moves us beyond where we are to where we want to be—past our pain and despair and discouragement to hope—an uncommon hope that leads to an uncommon life."

—Joe Wittwer, lead pastor of Life Center

"My friend Kurt is a fantastic example of trying to lead the authentic Christian and pastoral life. If you are looking for a book that reveals transparent truth focused on God and His Word, this would be a fantastic help in your journey to hope. Trust me, he's the real deal."

—Dan Shields, lead pastor of Valley Real Life

"Hope. We can't live without it, yet it often seems elusive. Kurt Bubna gives us an insightful and often humorous glimpse at holding onto hope regardless of how disheartened we may be."

—Dr. Kent Mankins, PhD, MEd, LMHC

BOOKS BY KURT W. BUBNA

Epic Grace:
Chronicles of a Recovering Idiot

Mr. and Mrs.:
How to Thrive in a Perfectly Imperfect Marriage:
A Christian Marriage Advice Book

Perfectly Imperfect:
A Devotional for Grace-Filled Living

The Rookie's Guide to Getting Published:
Survival Tips from the Trenches

Pete the Prodigal Pumpkin:
A Good News Halloween Story

Bye-Bye Monsters:
Facing Your Fear

Essential Life Press
Spokane, Washington
KurtBubna.com

Editing: Shayla Raquel, ShaylaRaquel.com
Cover Design & Interior Formatting: Melinda Martin, MelindaMartin.me

ISBN 978-0-9979891-1-3 (paperback)

This book is dedicated
to those who are sometimes restless or afraid,
to those who doubt,
and to those who struggle with life at times—
and that would be all of us.

CONTENTS

Chapter 1   Life Is Hard, But 1

Chapter 2   Why Are Relationships So Difficult?........................ 11

Chapter 3   Fear Knot! 21

Chapter 4   Shattered Hope 33

Chapter 5   No Longer in Eden.. 45

Chapter 6   Thirty-one Million Seconds 57

Chapter 7   Does My Life Matter?.. 69

Chapter 8   Running on Empty 79

Chapter 9   Turtles Are Not Mutant Ninjas.............................. 91

Chapter 10   Waiting Is Not for Wimps! 103

Chapter 11   Hope in the Face of the Unexpected...................... 115

Chapter 12   My Left Foot Has Been to Tibet............................. 127

Chapter 13   One Truly Is the Loneliest Number 137

Chapter 14   Infertility, Miscarriage, and Other Loss................. 147

Chapter 15   Buck Naked!... 157

Chapter 16   The Challenge of Influencing Children with Hope 171

Chapter 17   How to Survive the "C" Word.............................. 183

            Epilogue: The Long Journey to Hope 193

            Acknowledgments 197

            About the Author 199

ONE

LIFE IS HARD, BUT . . .

Our pain is never wasted.
—*Bob Goff*

If you're breathing, you're struggling. Maybe not with something world-shattering such as cancer or divorce, but life on this side of eternity is troublesome at times.

If you find that statement annoying or cynical, or if it's something you're not prepared to deal with at the moment, I understand. But you are probably upset because you're in the midst of hardship right now (and don't want to think about it), you're in denial, or somebody has convinced you to "positively confess" your way out of trouble.

I know it's challenging to read a book about hope when you're hopeless or pretending all is well, but maybe it's time to face the battle and grow through it.

For the record, I'm not a pessimist or a fatalist. However, after many decades of experience on planet Earth, I accept this reality: Life is hard, but that's not the end of the story.

By the way, Jesus agrees with me. He said, "In this world you will have trouble. But take heart! I have overcome the world."[1] Jesus isn't the preacher who tells you to put on a happy face despite your struggles and heartaches. He does, however, want us to refocus our angst by looking to Him and remembering His ultimate victory on our behalf.

Yep. Life isn't always easy, and it rarely meets all our expectations. Occasionally, our dreams become nightmares. Sometimes, our hopes get demolished by unexpected tragedies, like a wrecking ball razing a building. Often, we zig right with all our strength and life zags left with a vengeance.

When life hits the fan, we have a few options:

- Give up
- Throw up
- Suck it up
- Blow up
- Lock up
- Deny what's happening (Deny up?)
- Look up

I vote for looking up. By that, I mean refocus on a higher reality when faced with a depressing reality. If you just sighed, shook your head, and considered tossing this book in the trash, hold on. "Looking up" isn't some useless, religious, ridiculous cliché. I promise to avoid pathetic spiritual platitudes.

Nevertheless, looking up is the best option because it means you decide where you will fix your eyes, your mind, and your heart. Where you focus your attention matters. A lot.

Try something with me for a second. Put your hand right in front of your face and about three or four inches from your nose. First, focus on your hand. Besides getting a bit cross-eyed (and looking a little strange to those around you if you're in public), you'll notice that if you focus on your hand, that's pretty much all you see.

Now, do it again and focus your eyes beyond your hand. Weird,

---

1 John 16:33 (NIV).

huh? Your hand is still there, still in your face, and still a reality. However, now you've focused elsewhere, on a bigger reality, and you can see more. Far more. You can see beyond what's right in your face.

Looking up doesn't mean slapping a Jesus sticker on your problem. It doesn't mean you say some memorized words of prayer to the painfully silent heavens. I am not suggesting you get more faith, or that you learn to be a better *overcomer*. (I'm not a big fan of that word.) Looking up means choosing to see beyond the struggle that's in your face. Instead of getting cross-eyed, confused, angry, or depressed, you make a conscious decision to intentionally attach your soul to the One who loves you more than His own life.

A BEAUTIFUL YET BROKEN SOUL

Sarah was a beautiful young woman who was born with an incredible talent to run, and to run fast. She came from a good family. Lived in a good part of town. Went to a good school and a good church, and most everyone considered her a good girl.

Until she wasn't.

Sarah got pregnant out of wedlock at seventeen, and her whole world upended. Her dad rejected her and told her she'd have to move out before the baby came. He told Sarah he was using "tough love" to teach her a lesson. Her Christian academy kicked her out too. She was a senior who'd attended the school since kindergarten. The principal told her he was using tough love to teach all the other students a lesson. (Apparently, it was a lesson about how to be a self-righteous Pharisee who turns away a sinner rather than embracing and offering grace to the broken.) Sarah's hopes of getting a scholarship to run track for the University of Oregon were demolished as well.

This young, talented girl now felt hopeless. So desperate, in fact, that she made a plan to give up her baby for adoption and kill herself after her little boy was born. All Sarah saw were the problems. All she felt was despair and shame.

As part of the adoption process with the Christian agency she'd selected, Sarah met with a counselor for several sessions. The second time Sarah and her adoption counselor spoke, the woman asked her, "What are your plans after you place the baby with the Brown family?"

"I don't know," she lied.

Sarah knew what, how, and when she would end her life.

Then the counselor, sensing Sarah's misery and depression, said something that changed everything. "Sarah, God's not done with you yet. He still has a marvelous plan for your life. Your pregnancy wasn't His plan, but God never gives up on us and He has a way of taking our failures and messes and mistakes to make something beautiful in us."

Sarah thought, *My dad has rejected me. My school and Christian friends have shunned me. My church treats me like I'm a harlot. Why wouldn't God reject me too?*

But then, in a moment of God-given clarity, she saw beyond her hand—beyond the failure in her face—and she chose to refocus. Sarah took her eyes off everything and everyone else and realized, *God's not done with me yet.*

Nothing about her circumstances changed, but in that second, everything *in her* changed. A rising hope began to grow in her soul.

Sarah still gave her little boy, Christopher, to a couple who'd suffered from infertility for years. Then she finished high school, attended a local college, and eventually became an OB nurse.

And guess what? During her years employed at a Catholic hospital, Sarah has told quite a few laboring single moms, "Don't despair. Don't give up. God's not done with you yet!" She has shared her story with many other young women, and her hope now gives hope to others.

God delights in taking our ugly struggles and failures and making something beautiful out of the mess. The promise of His Word is that "every detail of our lives is continually woven together to fit into God's perfect plan of bringing good into our lives."[2] Redemption, restoration, and renewal are His specialties.

AT ONE TIME . . .

There was an extremely religious and self-righteous man named Saul, and he hated Christians. He saw them as an abomination and their beliefs as a gross aberration of the one true faith in Jehovah God.

To Saul, persecution, imprisonment, and murder by stoning of these fanatical Jesus followers were legitimate ways of ridding the world of this cancer called *the Way*. He was quite confident about his choices and path.

Until he wasn't.

As the story unfolds, Saul ends up having a life-changing encounter with the last person he ever expected to meet: Jesus.[3]

Here's the *Reader's Digest* version of what happened. Saul leaves Jerusalem with authorization from the religious leaders to capture any Christians he finds and drag them back to the Holy City. His first stop on his persecution tour is Damascus. However, just outside that city, he gets knocked on his butt by a bright light and he hears a voice saying, "What the Hades are you doing? Why are you persecuting me?" (*Unauthorized Bubna Paraphrase Version*).

Saul, stunned and now blinded by the light, asks, "What the what? Who are you?"

"I am Jesus, the Victorious, the one you are persecuting. Now, get up and go into the city, where you will be told what you are to do."[4]

Saul's traveling companions are baffled by all this because they heard the voice but didn't see anyone. So they took Saul by the hand and led him to Damascus.

Can you imagine how hopeless this religious bigot must have felt

---

2 Romans 8:28 (TPT).

3 Find the entire story in Acts 9.

4 Acts 9:7 (TPT).

after getting knocked to his knees by Jesus? Everything he'd believed was now upended.

Blind (for three days), Saul wouldn't eat or drink anything. I'm sure he was replaying in his mind the persecution and stoning of Stephen, which he once supported.[5] He was probably trying his best to drown out the terrified cries of the women and children he'd thrown into prison because they followed this crucified Rabbi wannabe named Jesus who confronted him on the road.

But then Saul has a vision about a man named Ananias who would come to pray for his healing. Ananias does precisely that, and Saul gets healed, baptized with the Holy Spirit, and baptized in water on the same day.

As the reality of his unjust and unfair persecution of Jesus's followers sinks in, I would not have blamed Saul if he blindly threw himself off a cliff in despair. I wouldn't have accused Ananias if he led Saul to the cliff and helped him jump! But Jesus caused Saul's eyes to refocus, and He gave this former murderous, self-righteous jerk a new purpose.

Make no mistake about it: Saul (later called Paul) lived a difficult life as the first Christian missionary. He summarized his many struggles and sufferings in a letter he wrote to the church in the city of Corinth.[6] He was thrown into prison, flogged, beaten, pelted with stones, shipwrecked, threatened by bandits and his fellow Jews, sleepless, hungry, cold, and naked at times.

Life was hard for Paul, but that's not the end of his story. He wrote nearly half of the New Testament, and his life has impacted billions of people. Billions.

Paul's difficulties became our blessings.

One of my favorites passages written by Paul is found in Titus 3:3–5 (NIV):

> At one time we too were foolish, disobedient, deceived and
> enslaved by all kinds of passions and pleasures. We lived in

5 See Acts 7.

6 2 Corinthians 11:16–33.

malice and envy, being hated and hating one another. But when the kindness and love of God our Savior appeared, he saved us, not because of righteous things we had done, but because of his mercy. He saved us through the washing of rebirth and renewal by the Holy Spirit.

At one time, Paul was a mess—not a hot mess, just a messy mess. He was a foolish, disobedient, deceived man who lived full of hate and malice toward Christians. But when Jesus showed up, everything changed. It's worth repeating: God delights in taking the failures of our lives to make something beautiful out of the stinky pile we created. I love the way Scott Sauls put it in his fantastic book, *Jesus Outside the Lines*: "Though they [people] are messed up now, Jesus has a plan to transform them into people who are glorious and guiltless."

God's specialty is redemption, restoration, and renewal.

MY MOST PAINFUL EXPERIENCE

In my first book, *Epic Grace: Chronicles of a Recovering Idiot*,[7] I told the heart-wrenching story of the death of my first grandson, Phineas Bubna.

On Saturday, March 15, 2008, my wife and I found out that our daughter-in-law was in premature labor—just seven months along—and that an ultrasound had indicated complications with the baby. We quickly packed, jumped in the truck, and drove as fast as we could from Spokane to Portland, where our kids lived. It was dark and rainy most of the way. Laura and I talked very little during those five hours on the road. We simply prayed. A lot.

About an hour outside of Portland, the cell phone rang. It was my son, Nathan. He could barely speak as he told us through his tears that his newborn son, Phineas, was gone. The little guy survived the delivery, and he was beautiful, but due to complications beyond anyone's

---

7 Published in 2013 by Tyndale Momentum.

control, and because his lungs were underdeveloped, he lived for less than an hour.

Laura and I pulled off the highway and just wept, more deeply than we had ever wept before or since. I wept for my son and his dear wife. I wept for my wife Laura and myself. I wept for Phineas. I had never known that kind of pain before. It was like a Mack truck was crushing my chest, and I couldn't breathe. It was unbearable.

When we walked into the hospital room an hour or so later, Nathan was holding his lifeless son, and the pain in his eyes broke my heart all over again. At that moment, I would have done anything to change what had happened. Without hesitation, I would have exchanged my own life for that of Phineas, if only I could have. I grabbed my son, and for one brief moment, father, son, and grandson embraced.

I kept thinking, *This isn't the way it's supposed to be. This isn't right. God, how could this be happening? No grandfather should outlive his grandson.*

For a long time, I agonized over this tragic loss to our family. God and I had some very long talks through tidal waves of tears. By God's grace, our family survived, but it took awhile for me to come to the place where I could fall on my face and worship.

In the weeks that followed Phineas's death, I learned that God could handle my pain and anger. He drew me very close and held me tight, even when I was confused and furious with Him. The depths of His grace sustained and carried me when all I wanted to do was crawl into a deep hole and hide.

I discovered that He really is "the God of all comfort."[8] He knows how hard it is to lose a Son, so He knows how best to encourage us through the agony of death and loss.

I also rediscovered the power of fixing my eyes on Jesus in the midst of great struggle. What I can never do, He has already done.

---

8 2 Corinthians 1:3 (NIV).

What is impossible for me in my strength is possible through God's grace.

I have told the story of the loss of Phineas to thousands and thousands. People cry. I still cry. I'm crying as I write this. But in that mysterious way that only God can do, my grandson's death has brought life and hope to many.

Some time ago, I received a short note from someone who read my book in prison. The man wrote, "Pastor Kurt, the story of your loss and yet your hope in God has given me new hope. If God can help you, He can help me. If God can get you through something like that, I know He can get me through my time in prison."

Phineas would be ten years old today, and I wonder what his personality would be like. What would he look like? What would he love to do? What would his laughter sound like? I sometimes ache when I think of Phineas and all that we've lost, yet hope is still rising out of our great pain.

God took a talented teenage girl who got pregnant, a busted religious bigot like Saul, and a heartbroken pastor like me, and He weaved the good, the bad, and the ugly into something mysteriously wonderful.

It is what God can do.

It's what He does best.

Remember, the death of Jesus was painful for the Father, but that wasn't the end of the story. And it's not the end of yours or mine, either.

EPIC STEPS

- Take an inventory of the major challenges in your life right now and decide to turn that list of struggles into a prayer list. Commit to do two things for the next thirty days with your list. First, give thanks to God every day for every one of your troubles. This is where you practice "giving thanks in all circumstances."[9] Second, ask at least one good friend to join you in prayer for these issues in your life.

- Take ten minutes to journal about at least one painful experience in your past when you have seen God redeem, restore, and renew you or others through it. This is where you remind yourself of God's goodness and power.

---

9 1 Thessalonians 5:16–18.

TWO

WHY ARE RELATIONSHIPS SO DIFFICULT?

*People tend to become
who we believe them to be
so let's believe the best.*

—Holley Gerth

"He's a contemptible and obnoxious idiot!"

"She let me down—again."

"My dad is so messed up that he thinks abnormal is normal. It's not. He's not!"

"I'm wondering what the return policy is on my kid. Every time we talk, I get so stinkin' mad!"

These are just a few of the comments people have made to me about their relationship struggles over the past couple of months. It's heartbreaking.

Yes, relationships often are incredible, but nothing shreds our souls more or depletes our hope faster than emotional turmoil with another person. Surviving life with a fractured human is challenging, discouraging, and sometimes enough to make us want to hurt someone.

Who in your life seems hopeless? Who makes you cringe and hit the ignore button on your phone when they call? Whether it's your spouse, your ex, your parent, your kid, your boss, or the person who wants-to-be-your-best-friend-but-you-don't-even-like-the-guy, all of us have an individual or two (or twenty) we'd rather live without. And in case you're wondering, that's normal and even part of God's plan to help you grow.

Hang in there. I'll explain how we grow in a bit. Before I do, let me tell you about my old friend Bob.

Bob is a narcissistic, egotistical, arrogant bonehead. Seriously.

I know that may seem harsh, but if you knew Bob, you'd probably come up with a few words to describe him that you can't use in a Christian book.

I first met Bob at a mutual friend's wedding over thirty years ago. I was with my young and beautiful wife. He was alone (in retrospect, no surprise). I wanted to sit at a table during the reception with some family and close friends. He wanted to find a table near the front and the dance floor where he could "make his splash" as he put it (i.e., be the center of attention).

Our table was full. There wasn't any room for Bob to sit with us, but that didn't stop him. He grabbed a chair from another table and squeezed himself in at our table right between my wife and me. I thought he was kidding around at first. He wasn't. Laura looked at me. I looked at her. She knew I wasn't beyond making some rude remark, so I got another look from her that said, "Don't make a scene. Just ignore him. Maybe he'll go away."

He didn't.

Not for over thirty years.

MERCY IS NOT MY NATURAL GIFT

I wish I could tell you that I'm naturally kind, understanding, and loving. However, patience with narcissists often eludes me. Especially with people who have no idea how to relate in socially acceptable ways or to play nice with others. Add to that a dash of stubbornness mixed with a pound of my pride, and you've got a recipe for trouble.

Over the years, that combination of my character weaknesses has made me incredibly intolerant of what I call VDPs—*very draining persons*. A more charitable person might call them EGRs—for *extra grace required*—or maybe not even label them at all (imagine that). But whatever you call them, the point is that they're not the most comfortable kind of people to hang out with, and they push my emotional buttons. Frequently.

It's sad but true; people are difficult sometimes. People can really tick us off and tweak our beaks. (Yes, I know, "tweaking" means something else now.) But God uses people, even people we'd rather avoid, to mold us and make us more like Him. It's not always pretty, and it's seldom easy, but it's good to have a Bob or two in our lives. Whether these VDPs bring out the worst or the best in our lives is up to us.

And oh, guess what? Everybody has at least one VDP in his or her life.

IT AIN'T PRETTY OR FUN

Tobi and Tom sat in my office in an emotional storm, much like a hurricane. One moment Tobi was cursing Tom, and the next she was bawling uncontrollably.

I understood. I knew Tom. I sympathized with her angst. I think Tom and Bob might be cousins.

About a decade earlier, Tobi and Tom met on a blind date, and neither one of them thought the other was marriage material. However, they both were willing to have some sexual fun before they moved on, so they did. Then something unexpected happened. Tobi got pregnant. Four months later, and four months before their daughter was born prematurely, they got married. It seemed the right and honorable thing to do. Just one problem: Their relationship started with sex, not friendship. He was not the prince she was waiting for, and she wasn't his princess, either.

Ten years and two more kids later, there's still no chemistry or fireworks between them. Tom hasn't held the same job for more than a year, and he spends more time at bars with his friends than he does at home. Their debt is quickly approaching the national debt of Paraguay. And now, to add insult to insult (which is worse than adding insult to injury), Tom got diagnosed with cancer. Their life and marriage went from "ain't no fun!" to "ain't no way!"

Tobi was done with Tom and their marriage.

Tom was suicidal.

On a side note, one thing that drives me crazy is having people show up in my office for marriage help after they've already given up. They wait too long after doing too little. I could be wrong, but it often seems like the couple is going through the motions of "we tried everything; we even got counseling from our pastor" so they can pull the plug with a little less guilt. At least, that was the intent behind Tobi and Tom's visit.

In between her ranting and wailing, Tobi said, "If God meant for us to be married, life would be easier! If we were meant to be together, life wouldn't be so f—— hard!"

Oh, boy. She dropped the F-bomb in my office. That can't be good.

Tom was nervous and sweating. Tobi was red-faced and fidgeting like a boxer waiting to pummel an opponent. I felt a bit like a baby rat about to get eaten by a really, really hangry snake.

I knew what I was about to say wasn't going to make me their favorite person.

"Uh, Tobi, who told you life and marriage would be easy? Who told you God's blessing means a life without struggle or hardship?"

At first, she glared at me with anger and fire in her eyes. It wasn't pretty. It wasn't fun. I wondered, for just a moment, if I could reach my office door to escape her wrath before she could catch me.

Then, the strangest thing happened. Tobi looked at Tom, looked back at me, and then sighed as she said, "Are you about to tell me *this* guy"—she pointed directly at him—"is God's will for my life?"

In one of my more brilliant pastoral moments, I asked, "What do *you* think? What has the Lord taught you about marriage?"

She knew.

I knew she knew.

People *always* know. They just don't want to know or don't want to accept what they already know.

"But why? Why do I have to stay with him? Why can't I just move on?"

"You can. God won't force you to do anything," I told her. "But marriage is holy, and it's one of God's best tools for shaping us into the image of His Son."

GOD'S CHISELS

Here's a crazy idea, one I want you to seriously consider for a moment: Could a part of God's plan for your spiritual, emotional, and relational growth be difficult people? Is it possible—maybe even the preferred pattern for development in your life—that God uses the person who irritates you the most to mature you?

One of my favorite authors, John Ortberg, put it this way: "Does my connection with this [difficult] person impact the person I'm becoming?"[10] In other words, are the annoying people in my life there to help me grow?

I think so. In fact, I know so.

I wrote this chapter at a Starbucks in Laguna Niguel, California. I was outside enjoying the sun, the palm trees, and, of course, the coffee. I love coffee. However, and I will put this delicately, java moves me. Typically, within an hour of my morning cup of joe, I need a restroom. Enough said.

---

10 John Ortberg, *I'd Like You More if You Were More like Me: Getting Real about Getting Close* (Illinois: Tyndale, 2017).

Fortunately, this Starbucks had two unisex restrooms. Unfortunately, one of them was out of order and the other occupied for a long time—too long. That was a problem since the person in the restroom was apparently sleeping. So, about every five minutes, I wiggled the handle. It was my not-so-subtle way of saying, "Other people are waiting, so please do your business and get out. Quickly. Thank you very much."

Fifteen minutes and three handle wiggles later, I finally hear the woman dwelling in the restroom say, with an extremely irritated and rude tone, "It's occupied!"

Duh. Believe me. I know.

It was bordering on ridiculous, and now becoming precarious. I made a strategic decision to walk (almost run) down the street to the Albertsons, thinking they must have a public restroom.

When I walked into the grocery store, I said to the first employee I saw, "Uh, excuse me, where's your bathroom?"

She laughed and said, "You're the eighth person in the last twenty minutes to ask me!"

"Yes, thank you for that not-so-helpful information, but I'm desperate. Where. Is. The. Restroom?"

"It's at the end of aisle one and to the left."

I rushed down the aisle, dutifully following her instructions, only to find she was directionally challenged—the restroom was to the right. Sigh.

Guess what I found when I entered the men's room? Two guys waiting in line for one toilet. Each looking as distressed as me.

My restroom dilemma was becoming a nightmare in the making, so I made another decision to leave Albertsons and bolt back to a Subway I had passed. When I entered the Subway, I rushed to the restroom door. It was locked and had a massive sign on the door that read, For the Use of Subway Customers Only. No Exceptions! Unbelievable.

Okay, I thought, *surely, the restroom at Starbucks is available by now.* So, I hurried back.

It was still occupied!

I wiggled the handle and knocked on the door. "Are you okay? Will you be much longer?" Finally, the door opened, and the same woman who'd yelled at me nearly twenty minutes earlier (and the scariest woman I've ever encountered) put her hands on her hips, stared at me, and scowled as she said, "I've been using the restroom. What's your problem?"

I snapped.

"My problem is you've been in there for over a half hour!"

At this point, and I kid you not, a Starbucks employee came up behind me and said, "You can use the other bathroom. It's okay now." She ripped the OUT OF ORDER sign off the other door.

Oh, my goodness! Relief and joy. Pure euphoria! I felt like I'd just found the lost city of Atlantis (pardon my underwater pun). I glared back at Restroom Lady and then used the other restroom.

As I washed my hands, I looked in the mirror and realized I was wearing a T-shirt from our church that said, LOVING GOD. LOVING PEOPLE. EASTPOINT CHURCH.

You've got to be kidding me. I just treated a complete stranger with contempt over her use, although abuse, of a public restroom.

Then the Holy Spirit whispered to my heart, "When you love others like Jesus, you put their needs before your own."

Busted.

And once again, I was given the opportunity to grow, to mature, and to become more like Jesus. Sadly, I failed the Starbucks restroom test, but if I'm anything, I'm an excellent repenter who learns from his mistakes.

WHAT IF?

What if you saw the challenging, annoying, and irritating people in your life as an opportunity to become more like Jesus? I'm not saying you live without boundaries or that you allow people to abuse you emotionally. That's never good.

I am saying, however, that every irritant is an opportunity for personal progress. As Lucretia Berry once wrote, "Sometimes what we learn in the midst of a struggle is the reward." And I assure you, it is possible to develop uncommon hope despite some very uncool people in your life.

Without question, every one of you has at least one VDP in your world. It could be your spouse, your child, your boss, your neighbor, or all of the above. There's no denying or avoiding this reality: Some relationships are difficult.

Welcome to planet Earth.

I suggest you stop complaining, stop wishing for an easier life, and start growing. A change in your perspective leads to uncommon hope even in the toughest relationships. Some people come into your life as a blessing. Some come into your life as a lesson. Either way, it's good.

Will it be easy?

Nope.

Will it be worth it?

Absolutely. I promise.

VDPs can be *very developmental people* in your life, because "our pressures will develop in us patient endurance. And patient endurance will refine our character, and proven character leads us back to hope."[11]

---

11 Romans 5:3–4 (TPT).

EPIC STEPS

- Who is a VDP or EGR in your life right now (i.e., the person who irritates you the most)? Take a moment to reflect on how that person is helping you to become more like Jesus. (Hint: Check out the fruits of the Spirit: love, joy, peace, forbearance, kindness, goodness, faithfulness, gentleness, and self-control.)[12]

- Ask God to help you see difficult people as His spiritual chisel; in fact, thank God for His commitment to maturing you into the image of Jesus.

---

12 Galatians 5:22–23 (NIV).

THREE

FEAR KNOT!

Never let a stumble in the road be the end of the journey.
—*Anonymous*

F ear is like a tattoo on our souls, except it's a mark we don't want anybody to see.

Fear and hope conflict with each other in our hearts. It's nearly impossible to believe and trust God when fear consumes our hope and hits us like a tidal wave out of nowhere. Everyone experiences the emotion of fear, but that doesn't help us feel any better about our own.

Most of us can easily think of the moments we've lived in absolute terror. For some, it could be a car wreck or a dog bite or a near-death experience.

For me, it's the dentist. I hate the dentist. Actually, I don't hate the person; I hate the experience. I have more fillings and root canals than most people have teeth. I'm pretty sure I've put a few of my dentist's kids through college.

The entire experience is a nightmare for me. Of course, the minions who serve Dr. Toothenstein try to pull the wool over my eyes. The room is clean, and the music is soothing. Everybody smiles and treats me like I'm about to go for a quiet walk on a beautiful beach. I'm placed in a recliner, of sorts, but just out of sight is a tray of neatly organized torture devices waiting to rip into my mouth. The doc enters with a sadistic grin. He asks how I'm doing while washing the evidence of his previous victim from his hands. I'm thinking, *If this is so safe, then why are they covering my eyes with safety glasses?* They can't fool me; in fact, as the chair reclines, every sinew of my body tenses up as if I'm about to be waterboarded.

Being a manly man (meaning proud and stubborn), I've typically said *no* to using any happy gas (nitrous oxide) during my visits to the dentist. But that all changed after spending three hours in an endodontist's chair in the summer of 2012. As she carved deeper and deeper into my jaw, trying to remove an obstinate root, I went deeper and deeper into a dark hole of terror. Frankly, I had my first panic attack, and I felt foolish, embarrassed, and angry with myself. It was one of the most terrifying experiences of my life.

FEAR SUCKS

Can you remember the last time you were afraid? Maybe it was a horrible encounter with a venomous snake while hiking. Perhaps it was at thirty thousand feet when your plane hit an air pocket, and you hadn't paid attention to the "keep your seat belt fastened at all times" warning, and suddenly your head was jammed into an air vent. Possibly it was during a movie such as *World War Z* or *A Quiet Place*, and you still wake up in the middle of the night screaming.[13] (I shrieked like a baby pig in both of those movies.)

Whatever your last fear experience was, I'm sure it still makes your pulse race and your heart skip a beat when you think about it.

Fear is like a vise grip on our minds. Terror puts our guts into knots of anguish. It squeezes our hearts. It hurts our faith. It wounds our souls. It's like getting punched in the solar plexus because it takes our breath away.

---

13 *World War Z* is a 2013 apocalyptic zombie film starring Brad Pitt; *A Quiet Place* is a 2018 American post-apocalyptic horror film directed by John Krasinski.

I understand. I've been there many times—way too many times. And whether your standard response to terror is fight or flight, either way it's embarrassing, isn't it? Let me tell you about one of my most humiliating experiences.

A NOT-SO-HOLY EXPERIENCE

Besides the dentist, I have a fear of small, dark confined spaces. (My blood pressure is rising just thinking about it.) I refuse to admit that I'm claustrophobic, but I'd rather die than be bound by duct tape and thrown into a small enclosed space. One study indicates that anywhere from 5 to 7 percent of the world's population is affected by severe claustrophobia.[14] That's 350 million or so people who will do *anything* to avoid a crowded elevator. I am one of them.

Some time ago, I had the experience of a lifetime. My mom and I went on a self-guided tour of the Holy Land (meaning I drove the car, and she drove me crazy with her directions). We visited everything from the Dead Sea to the Old City of Jerusalem. It was an incredible trip.

One afternoon, I decided to visit Hezekiah's Tunnel. King Hezekiah dug a tunnel underneath the City of David in ancient times. He created this 1,750-foot channel in the mountain to provide water for Jerusalem before an impending siege by his enemy, the Assyrians.[15] Trekking through this underground passageway in knee-deep water is a highlight for many visitors to Jerusalem.

The day before, I'd gone to check it out, but hundreds of students were in line and the wait was too long. When I returned the following day, I was surprised to find almost no one in line for a ticket. I thought, *Cool! I can get through this in no time and without any crowds.*

---

14 Wikipedia, s.v. "Claustrophobia," last modified September 16, 2019, http://en.wikipedia.org/wiki/Claustrophobia.

15 See 2 Kings 20:20.

Wrong. What was I thinking? It's a small, tight, and dark tunnel! As it turned out, it was one of the worst moments of my life.

Only three things are required for this tunnel-of-death expedition: water-worthy shoes, a flashlight, and nerves of steel. What the heck—two out of three ain't bad, right?

After paying my twenty shekels, I entered the security gate and began my descent. Keep in mind, I'm alone, my mom is back at the hotel resting, and my only companion is a pathetic penlight as I go far below the surface of the earth—down what seemed like thousands of steps.

So far, so good. However, I did pause at one moment and wonder: *What if my battery dies or I drop my flashlight?* That would be bad. Really bad. Then my mind started going a bit wonky. *What if there's an earthquake? What if there's a terrorist attack? What if somebody drops a bomb on Jerusalem and I'm trapped down here for days or weeks? What if Jesus comes back and I'm too deep to get raptured?*

Boldly (or foolishly), I pressed on deeper and deeper into the abyss. I finally hit the bottom of the steps and entered through a small opening into the actual water-filled tunnel. The water felt refreshing, but complete darkness now surrounded me. I found myself confined by rock walls that seemed to squeeze the air out of my lungs.

I started to panic. *There's probably very little oxygen down here! I bet this water is filthy! What if I never see my wife and kids again?!*

I'm not proud of the way I felt. Being alone was a mixed blessing. On the one hand, I was glad no one was there to see me lose it, but I would have held a complete stranger's hand if only someone, anyone, were present. I'm not sure how far I got before I turned around and ran back to the steps toward freedom.

Immediately as I exited the tunnel, two couples greeted me. In fact, I surprised them as I bolted out of the passageway like a bullet. I'm sure I looked like a ghost, and the woman in the back of this small group said, "There's no way in h—— I'm going in there!" I nodded my heartfelt agreement, grunted something about death by darkness, and ran past them up the stairs and to the nearest exit. The moment I burst into the sunlight, it was like hearing the "Hallelujah Chorus" for the first time. I was moved to tears! For real.

Fear sucks. Physically, emotionally, mentally, and experientially, it robs us of so much.

Even if you are an adrenaline junky who loves doing crazy things solely for the rush, you'd still have to admit that fear can kill you. On the good-bad scale of things, fear is evil unless it's used for good. Meaning, unless you have a reasonable fear that keeps you from doing unreasonable things, fear is bad. Sometimes tragically bad.

THE THING ABOUT FEAR

I have a rational fear of grizzly bears, so when I hike in any national park, I make a lot of noise. I have a sensible fear of the IRS, so I don't cheat on my taxes. I have a reasonable fear of little old ladies driving ancient and massive cars, so I give a wide berth to headless vehicles. Not all fears are evil or to be avoided.

It's the *unreasonable* fears I'm addressing:

- The fear of flying, although you're far more likely to die in a car crash.

- The fear of insects that you can crush under your heel.

- The fear of the dentist, even though he or she is a trained professional seeking to alleviate your pain, not cause more of it.

- And of course, the fear of darkness and confined spaces like Hezekiah's Tunnel, when the tunnel is probably one of the safest places in all of Israel.

Unfounded fears produce unnecessary reactions that cripple us and cause us to withdraw from living the epic life God has planned for us. Too often we say *no* to God-given opportunities because we're afraid. Too often we miss the chance to develop and grow because we've chosen to play it safe and avoid any risks.

For years, I was terrified to speak in front of a crowd. It didn't matter if it was a classroom of peers and friends or an auditorium of strangers. It was an unreasonable fear, and it kept me from discovering a gift of teaching that God had given to me. No one was going to stone me for stumbling over a word or boo me off the stage if I stuttered, but I still let the fear of public speaking keep me from something I was made to do.

I have a dear friend who is a germophobe. Admittedly, I avoid sick people and never practice the five-second rule even when I drop my favorite food on the floor, but she avoids people almost to the point of isolation. She is a kind, wise, and talented woman whom the world should know, but her fear keeps her in hiding.

The problem with fear is it costs us when it controls us. It steals precious time. It wastes our energy. It often robs us of our destiny, and it destroys our hope.

Jesus told a parable recorded in Matthew 25 that illustrates the problem of fear. In the story, the boss gave bags of gold (aka, talents) to three of his employees. The first guy got three bags, the second person received two, and the third only one bag, "each according to his ability."[16] The first two were diligent, worked hard, and doubled what they had. The third was afraid, so he buried his gold, hid his talent, and in the end, he earned nothing and then lost what he'd been given.

The principle? Good and faithful people take risks, overcome fear, and effectively use what has been graciously given to them by God. In other words, don't bury your talents because you're afraid of failure. Use them or lose them.

---

16 See Matthew 25:14–30.

VOICE OF AN ANGEL

When Ashley sang, she had the voice of an angel. Her natural ability to play multiple instruments made three-chord guitar players like me jealous. She wrote songs that moved me. I could sit and listen to her all day, every day, and be lost for hours by her musical genius. She was truly gifted.

Anybody who knew Ashley knew she had a God-given ability. There was merely one problem: She wouldn't sing or play for people she didn't know, like, or trust. She suffered from debilitating insecurity. If you weren't family or a very good friend, Ashley wouldn't perform for you. It was her way or no way, so her gift was buried beneath her fears.

Ashley was afraid. Afraid of rejection. Afraid to fail. Afraid to end up somewhere she didn't want to be with expectations she might not be able to fulfill. She was afraid of not being in control. Fear kept this woman and her incredible gift from the world.

Last I heard, Ashley was working for a dry cleaner and her gifts are still hidden. She still sings from time to time, but her only audience is empty suits and pressed shirts. What a tragic waste.

Sometimes I find myself whistling or singing one of her tunes. Like a wine stain on my heart, her songs have become a part of me, not easily removed or forgotten. I drift to her music without even thinking about it, but when I realize what I'm doing, I become terribly sad.

Most of us have someone in our lives who amazes us. We watch that person with awe. We might even secretly envy his or her gifts.

If only I could sing like that . . .

If only I were that smart or talented or . . .

If only . . .

Perhaps it's time to focus on what you already have rather than on what you wish you had, or you, too, might end up with wasted potential. Maybe you're afraid you don't have enough or don't measure up to others. Lots of us are deathly afraid of failure, so we cower under the sheets saying, "I wish I could, but . . ." Fear kills faith, obliterates hope, and paralyzes us in our imagined safety zone.

In her book, *Love Idol*, Jennifer Dukes Lee writes, "Fear has a way of carrying God-planted dreams into dark corners while the Accuser hisses a single, debilitating word: *Coward*."[17]

We all know what it takes to grow. We understand the need to step through the fear threshold that's holding us back. Yet all too often, we shrink back and listen to the thief who came to "steal and kill and destroy."[18] We let go of the dream and the assurance of abundant-life-to-the-max because we're terrified of the bogeyman in our closet.

Here's an idea: Let's drag the monster (real or imagined) out of the darkness and into the light of God's presence and promise. Let's face our fears and reveal them for what they are: beliefs or acts of faithlessness that often lead to hopelessness.

If God is faithful (and He is), then what have we to fear? David, after being seized by his enemy, the Philistines, wrote, "When I am afraid, I put my trust in You."[19] I love the fact that the man who killed Goliath admitted his battle with fear. He said, "*When* I am afraid . . ." He didn't deny his fear, but he didn't stop there, either. "When I'm freaking out . . . I will put my confidence and hope in You."

FEAR IS BIG. GOD IS BIGGER.

I'm the last guy on the planet to give you a hard time about being afraid. I get it. If you struggle with fear, I'm your brother from another mother. You'll get no finger-wagging or shaming looks from me. But we don't have to stay stuck in the grip of terror. We can live free. We can grow. But like most spiritual growth, it probably won't come easy.

If you've ever tried to untangle a ball of Christmas tree lights, you

---

17 Jennifer Dukes Lee, *Love Idol: Letting Go of Your Need for Approval and Seeing Yourself through God's Eyes* (Illinois: Tyndale Momentum, 2013).

18 John 10:10 (NIV).

19 Psalm 56:3 (NIV).

know how frustrating it is to struggle with a mess of knots. I've come pretty close to losing my sanity right in front of the plastic baby Jesus sitting on my fireplace mantel. Without a doubt, the angel on top of my tree has snickered at me many times as I endeavored to unravel the not-so-holy lights of Christmas.

Fear in your soul is like that: a tangled, messy mass. But here's the thing: You can choose to "fear not" rather than live bound by "fear knots."

But to live free, we need to consider a few things:

First, we need a change in our perspective. This life is temporary. Our bodies are "but dust,"[20] and we're scheduled for an upgrade in eternity. When we remember that Jesus defeated death,[21] it can change the way we view our fears.

Second, we need a change in our minds. Fear is often the result of faulty thinking. We develop destructive mental habits that become emotional ruts. I heard someone once say, "You fight bad thoughts with good thoughts." I couldn't agree more. We must teach our minds to dwell on whatever is excellent and admirable and to focus our thoughts on all that is true, holy, just, pure, lovely, and worthy of praise.[22] The Bible also says, "You will keep in perfect peace all who trust in you, all whose thoughts are fixed on you!"[23] In other words, a God-fixed mind is a peace-filled mind.

We also need to train ourselves to pray and seek God when terror strikes. I love these words of David, found in the Psalms: "I sought the LORD, and he answered me; he delivered me from all my fears."[24]

When the unexpected happens (and it will), to whom do you turn first? Does your heart run toward God in prayer, or do you run to the medicine cabinet for a Valium?

---

20 Psalm 103:14.

21 See 1 Corinthians 15.

22 Philippians 4:8.

23 Isaiah 26:3 (NLT).

24 Psalms 34:4 (NIV).

Prayer is powerful. Prayer takes us to the One who is able to rescue us. Prayer shifts our focus from the earthly to the heavenly. The apostle Paul wrote this to the church: "Do not be anxious about anything, but in every situation, by prayer and petition, with thanksgiving, present your requests to God. And the peace of God, which transcends all understanding, will guard your hearts and minds in Christ Jesus."[25]

Peter challenged us to cast all our anxiety on God because He cares for us.[26] Years ago, I had a little placard on my wall that read PRAYER CHANGES THINGS. And it does, because prayer changes *us*.

Finally, we must learn to lose our fears in the sea of God's love. In many ways, the root of all fear is spiritual. We doubt the goodness of God. We question the love of Jesus. We wonder if God is indeed mindful of us and our situation. But "perfect love casts out fear."[27] Knowing we are deeply loved by a Father who always has our best interest at heart is critical to living an epic life.

What might have changed in that tunnel or the endodontist's chair if I had turned to God in prayer and chosen to fix my attention on Him? Would remembering all of His goodness and love in my life have changed my terror into triumph?

I imagine I will wrestle with some fears for the rest of my life, but I cannot afford to let them control me or my destiny in Christ. The key for you and me is to press beyond them and to walk through the fear threshold before us. Why? Because an epic life beyond our wildest imagination is waiting for us on the other side of the fear barrier.

The tunnel you're in might be pitch-black, and you may believe you're all alone. Terrifying circumstances in your life might make you feel as if a boa constrictor has wrapped its body around your chest and neck. I wish there was a magic wand you could wave to make all your fears disappear. I feel your pain. I truly do.

Nonetheless, here's what I know: What and Whom we choose to

---

25 Philippians 4:6–7 (NIV).

26 1 Peter 5:7.

27 1 John 4:18 (ESV).

focus on has everything to do with us overcoming fear, stepping out in faith, and experiencing the abundant, uncommon, hope-filled life God has planned for us.

Why would we settle for anything less?

EPIC STEPS

- Take ten minutes to journal about the last time you were truly afraid. What happened? Why were you terrified? Was your fear rational or irrational? Was it reasonable or unreasonable? Have there been any residual effects in your life because of that experience?

- Where has fear held you back from an epic life? How has the loss of hope trapped you into an unhealthy mind-set? Have you buried any God-given "treasure" (i.e., talents) in your life due to fear of failure?

- List some of your biggest fears. Now, take a moment and ask yourself, "Are any of my fears bigger than God and His power?" If the answer is *no*, and of course it is, then pick just one fear and decide today to push through the fear barrier into faith.

FOUR

SHATTERED HOPE

God writes straight on crooked lines.
—Anonymous

I love a good story, especially one in which God chooses to use the young and the hopeless.

In the first chapter of Jeremiah, God interrupted Jerry's young life with a radical challenge: "I'm choosing you to shake up this world. In fact, this is precisely why you were born! I'm going to use your life and words to pull up, tear down, take apart, and demolish the old, and then we'll start over by building and planting what I desire."

In utter shock, Jerry replied, "But, God, I don't know anything. I'm terrified of public speaking! Besides, I'm just a teenager, and no one is going to listen to me."[28]

Before you judge this kid too harshly, I wonder how many times you've said, "But, God . . ." as you've offered up your seemingly reasonable excuses for why something simply cannot be done by you.

But, God, that's impossible!

But, God, people will think I'm crazy!

But, God, I'm a mess!

But, God, that's not in my wheelhouse of experience or gifts.

---

28 Bubna Paraphrase of the biblical book of Jeremiah 1.

We are quick to point out the apparent absurdity of God's expectations. Most of us have a finely tuned this-is-ridiculous meter that tends to function quite well when set off by the unexpected.

We don't have to dig very deeply to find a reason to say *no* to God. Why? Because we are painfully aware of our past failures, our present weaknesses, and the future likelihood of repeating the same mistakes we've always made. We choose to believe that God can't use us because we're not strong enough, smart enough, or good enough.

Here's something I need you to embrace and remember: Our past shapes us, but it doesn't have to define us or control us. Our history influences our future, but it shouldn't imprison us. In Christ, we are more than the sum of our past mistakes.

I bet I've had a thousand conversations with people who reject the idea of experiencing a hopeful and meaningful life because of their epic failures. They don't think about what might be possible in their lives because they can't get past the things they've done or get beyond their real or perceived inadequacies. The list of their sins is mammoth and crushing: abuse, adultery, deceit, drug addiction, hate, porn, and the list goes on. Even if you're feeling fairly smug after reading *that* list, perhaps you've lied, cheated on your taxes, gossiped, or run a red light or two.

We'll take a look at our common human condition more in the next chapter, but here I want to address our tendency to bail on God and disqualify ourselves because of failure.

"COACH, I NEED TO HAVE AN ABORTION"

I coached track and cross-country at the high school level for many years. As a marathoner and avid runner once upon a time, I enjoyed inspiring a younger generation to fall in love with the simplicity and purity of running. If I hadn't become a pastor, I probably would have become a high school teacher. Working with students was always a great joy.

One miserable spring day in the first hour of track practice, we experienced rain, hail, and high winds. The kids hated days like this, and so did their coaches. When the lightning started up, it was time to send everyone home. It's one thing to run as fast as lightning but quite another to get hit by it. It's scary how a javelin pointing skyward works as a lightning rod.

One girl, Emily, went to the bleachers instead of the locker room.[29] I had noticed that she seemed distracted at practice that day. She sat down in the stands and buried her face in her hands.

As a coach, I had learned early on that young women can be a bit moody at times. They go through all sorts of physical and emotional changes. They fall in love, have their hearts broken, and then fall in love again, so it's sometimes difficult to keep them focused on their performance at practice. I know, guys can be emotional too, but most are too macho to show it publicly.

I figured Emily was wrestling with something minor in the grand scheme of things, but I thought I'd better check on her just in case. As I approached her, I discovered she was sobbing. In fact, I've rarely seen anyone cry so hard. Frankly, I wasn't sure if I should leave her alone or ask if there was anything I could do, but I knew I had to say something.

I sat down next to her on the bleachers. "Emily, are you okay?" (First stupid question.)

Now she was rocking and wailing uncontrollably.

"Hey, are you upset?" (Second stupid question. Women might be emotional at times; guys are just clueless.)

I wanted to put my arm around her to comfort her, but as a male coach alone with her in the grandstands, I needed to be wise. So, I just sat there patiently and waited for her to come up for air. After a few minutes, with her face still buried in her trembling hands, she said, "Coach, I don't know what to do. I need to have an abortion." Then

---

29 Pseudonym.

she let out a cry so loud that anyone within a hundred yards would have heard it.

My heart sank. I'd heard this from other women before but never from a fifteen-year-old. For heaven's sake, one of my daughters was her age. At that point, I was choking back my own tears. But what she said next will forever haunt me. "Coach, my life is over. I've f—— things up so bad I know God hates me. Nothing will ever be okay again."

Being a man, a coach, and a pastor, my natural inclination is to fix things. If it's broken, I can repair it. If an answer is needed, I can find one. If you want some wise counsel, the doctor is in. But what do you say to a young woman who's suicidal over her poor life choices? As she rocked back and forth, sobbing over and over again, Emily kept saying, "I just want to die. I should just take some pills and die."

Her parents didn't know she was pregnant. Her friends had no idea. She didn't have a pastor—just a coach she trusted because she knew I cared about her.

I took a deep breath, put my hand on her shoulder, and gently whispered, "We've all made horrible mistakes in our lives, and things do change, but God *never* hates us, Emily. He's not mad at you. He's weeping *with* you. When your heart is broken, His heart is broken too."

We spent the next thirty minutes talking. I listened as Emily poured out her heart. I learned a lot about her in that short time. The one thing I know Emily heard from me was that God can forgive us of anything. I assured her, "God's not mad *at* you. He's mad *about* you, and He still has a good plan for your life. Restoration is His specialty."

Emily never ended her life, and she chose not to have an abortion, but sadly she did miscarry. (And that painful experience took her through another round of guilt.) However, years later, she emailed me and said, "Coach, no one ever encouraged me like you did that day not to give up. No one ever told me I am loved by God no matter what. I'm still not sure how I feel about this whole following Jesus thing, but I think you showed me what Jesus is like that day."

I wept when I read her email. My heart aches for so many who know so little about the uncommon and amazing hope God offers.

Like this young woman, many of us feel we've gone too far and failed too miserably to ever get back on track. Even if God once had a great plan for our lives, we believe it's too late now. But avoiding epic failure is not a prerequisite to experiencing a hope-filled life.

We're all in trouble if the path to hope and purpose in Christ requires perfection. We must learn to get past what we've done and get beyond our glaring inadequacies. God is bigger than our foolishness. He can redeem, restore, and renew any life that is fully surrendered to Him.

A DREAM CHANGED EVERYTHING

I read a moving story some time ago about Bashir Mohammad.[30] He was once a member of Al-Qaeda who hated Christians and said, "I would have slaughtered anyone who suggested [Christianity]" as a way of life.

Eventually, he became disillusioned as he saw Muslims killing Muslims, and he left the fighting to go to Turkey with his wife, Rashid. It was there that his young wife became seriously ill. Desperate for help, Bashir asked his cousin Ahmad for help. However, when he discovered that his cousin was a Christian, he decided to look for assistance elsewhere. That attempt didn't work out. So, without any-where else to turn, Bashir reached out to his cousin again, who asked a Christian prayer group to sing over and pray for his wife. She rapidly recovered!

Rashid's quick recovery stunned Bashir and triggered interest in Jesus for both him and Rashid. Not too long after that, a preacher in

---

30 Faithwire, Stephanie Parker, "Modern Day Paul? Jihadist Who Once Terrorized Christians and Muslims Has a MAJOR Conversion," March 28, 2017, https://www.faithwire.com/2017/03/28/modern-day-paul-jihadist-who-once-terrorized-christians-and-muslims-has-a-major-conversion.

Istanbul opened their eyes to the gospel. Interestingly, a dream about Jesus meeting his needs sealed the deal for Bashir, as he felt deeply loved by Jesus during his dream.

Today, Bashir and his wife hold a Christian service in his Istanbul home where he cares for twenty-two other Christian refugees.

Why do I love this story? Because if God can take a Christian-hating Muslim, redeem him, and then use him to lead others to Christ, then He can do anything with you and me.

A BIG DILEMMA

We tend to see God through our shattered perspective, and that's a big problem. With a severely damaged self-image, we generally have a broken God-image too. In fact, let's be honest: Some of us believe God is great and all-powerful, but we can't imagine Him doing anything astonishing through *our* lives. We sing worship songs about His awesomeness, but we believe God is limited in what He can do with screwups like us.

A considerable part of the dilemma is that we like to create gods in our image. We make gods out of the rich and famous. We elevate leaders (including politicians and pastors) to godlike status. We put them on a pedestal somewhere prominent in our lives, but in the end, it's a puny little god we've made to worship rather than the Almighty God. Sadly, if our God is too tiny or too human (like we are), then our faith and confidence in Him will be too small as well.

Deep down, we want to believe that God can do anything, but we're pretty sure He has limits when it comes to us. Time or space might not constrain God, but a craftsman is only as good as the material he has to work with, right?

And we know what we are.

More mud than marble.

More sandstone than diamond.

More broken than whole.

In case you're wondering, I'm not a big fan of self-confidence. Despite what the positive-thinking gurus have to say, I'm *not* okay (and neither are you). I can sit in a lotus position for hours chanting, "I am good. I am awesome. My life force in the universe matters. I am good. I am awesome. There is nothing I can't do." But in my gut, I know I'm not that good. In fact, I know I'm pretty messed up at times.

So, what's the alternative to emotional self-flogging or self-confident bragging? The substitute for self-confidence is God-confidence. In other words, I must put my confidence and hope in God and His ability to accomplish anything even through an imperfect, broken guy like me.

The god I've created in my mind has limits. The God of the universe does not.

I am broken. He is not.

Working with people who are demoted to the scratch-and-dent pile of life is His specialty.

I WISH I COULD, BUT . . .

A few years ago, I had coffee with a middle-aged man in our church. Tony was gifted and full of potential. However, I noticed that he'd stayed in the shadows and refused to get involved. When I asked him why, he replied, "Oh, I wish I could serve, but I'm divorced."

I was flabbergasted. "Who told you divorced means disqualified?"

He took the next twenty or so minutes to tell me his story. He and his first wife married young. Neither one of them was a Christ follower during their marriage. They both came from broken and dysfunctional homes deeply bound by sexual sins. Sadly, during their ten-year marriage, both of them had multiple affairs. The fact that their marriage had survived beyond a year or two surprised everybody who knew them. Eventually, they "fell out of love" (I hate that phrase) and went their separate ways.

A few years later, after another failed marriage and two DUIs,

Tony hit rock bottom and ended up in AA. His sponsor was the first person ever to tell Tony about Jesus. Eventually, he became a devout follower of Christ, and within another year or so, he married a godly woman who loved Jesus with all her heart.

He was Lutheran when they got married. She was active in the Church of Christ. Neither one of them felt comfortable in the other's denomination, so they decided to start fresh at a new charismatic church in their neighborhood. After just a few months, their pastor told them, "You are welcome to attend our church, but you can't serve here since you are living in sin." According to this pastor's theology, anyone who divorced for anything other than adultery and remarries another is living in an unforgivable state of sin.

With tears in his eyes, Tony said to me, "We had no idea that God saw our marriage as a mistake and sinful, but we couldn't divorce each other. If that means we can't serve God, so be it." Then they left that church in humiliation.

As Tony told me his story, I went from being dumbfounded to being mad (I'd say pissed, but that word is offensive to my momma)! How could anyone tell this man he was disqualified because of sin that had happened *before* he was a Christ follower? I grabbed my Bible and went pastoral on him. With a passion that surprised him, I assured this brother that he did not need to live as a second-class Christian.

Maybe you've read this verse: "Anyone who belongs to Christ has become a new person. The old life is gone; a new life has begun!"[31] Or perhaps you're familiar with Paul's words to Titus: "He [God] saved us, not because of the righteous things we had done, but because of his mercy. He washed away our sins, giving us a new birth and new life through the Holy Spirit."[32]

I looked Tony in the eye and said, "Buddy, *everything* that happened BC (before Christ) is gone! New birth and new life mean a new start, and we are *never* disqualified by what we did before we surren-

---

31 2 Corinthians 5:17 (NLT).

32 Titus 3:5 (NLT).

dered our lives to Jesus! In fact, the blood of Jesus covers all our sins, including the ones we committed after becoming a Christian. If we've confessed it and repented of it, no past sin can rob us of our destiny or disqualify us from service in God's kingdom!"[33]

It was his turn to be dumbstruck. It was as if the heavens had parted and he heard the voice of God saying, "You are my beloved son, and I am well pleased with you." Is divorce a sin? Often it is, but it's *not* an unpardonable sin.

I'm pleased to tell you that Tony and his wife still serve at Eastpoint, and God continues to surprise and delight them with His uncommon hope and amazing grace.

Why do we so easily doubt the goodness of God?

Why do we listen to the gloomy voices of the self-righteous or the dark voice of the accuser?

Why are we so quick to disqualify ourselves because of past failures?

BETWEEN THE CROSS AND EASTER

If anyone ever felt ineligible for future greatness, it would have been the first disciples of Jesus. Every one of them had abandoned Jesus on the night Judas betrayed Him. In His moment of need, they all ran. Some, like Peter, swore they didn't even know Him; others hid in the shadows, but they all sinned. I can only imagine the guilt and shame that consumed them.

The Saturday after the crucifixion was a horrible day for these troubled men. We see it as the period between the cross and Easter, but at the time, they didn't see it that way or understand what we know in hindsight.

The Jewish Sabbath was typically a day of rest, but this Saturday was a time of gut-wrenching heartache. The disciples' teacher, Rabbi, Lord, and closest friend lay dead in a stone tomb. Their dream of a

---

33 1 John 1:9; Titus 3:3–7.

Messiah-led rebirth of Israel was crushed. All hope of a Jewish revival was now completely shattered.

The disciples feared for their own lives as they cowered in an upper room somewhere in the city of Jerusalem. Overnight, they had become religious outcasts among the very people who once had sung the praises of Jesus and His motley crew.

These men and women who loved Jesus experienced a dreadfully dark and demoralizing day. In their minds, He was gone forever, and they were, in part, to blame.

On the Friday of Jesus's crucifixion, they had run, they had denied, they had watched from a distance in horror, and they had wept in agony. On Saturday, they lived in shock, dread, and dark corners of deafening silence.

Remember, they didn't understand the promise of Easter or the hope of the resurrection.

Not yet.

Not on *that* day.

It was the second worst day of their lives, and from their limited perspective, they would never have a good day again.

I wonder how many of you are in a similar place.

Something inside you has died. You've lost a dream, a relationship, a job or a friend, and you're exhausted. In fact, you're an emotional and physical wreck. Numbness covers your heart, mind, and soul like a dense winter fog. You can't even think about the future. The misery of yesterday and the emptiness of today have stolen from you any joy or hope for a better tomorrow.

Perhaps you often drift in your mind to some horrible past sin. Maybe you're devoured by your failure and overwhelmed by your foolishness. If that's you, please listen to these words: God knows where you've been, where you are, and where He will take you. He understands the crushing anguish of sin that led Jesus to the cross for us, but He also knows (far better than you do) that Sunday is coming. And it will be a brand-new day.

The Friday of the crucifixion was devastating to the hope of Jesus's followers. Saturday was the second darkest day of the disciples' lives as they grieved over both their loss and their failures. But Sunday changed everything. Sunday was a day of uncommon and restored hope!

God knows your past, present, and future, but He sees a sunrise of hope on the horizon. Simply confess your sin and rest in His grace so you can live free and forgiven. Let go of the things you can't change about your past and trust God with your present and your future. Stop making excuses, walk in forgiveness, and don't let your regrets become a reason to opt out of hope or live an epic life in Christ.

God is bigger than your past and greater than your sins. And you can live with no excuses and no regrets when you realize that God never wastes anything or any life that is fully surrendered to Him.

So, hold on.

Stay true.

Don't despair.

Don't give up.

Sunday is just around the corner.

EPIC STEPS

- How, perhaps, have you allowed your past to define or control you? (Again, history does shape us, but it doesn't need to trap us.) Be honest as you write down one or two areas in your life where you feel stuck in the past.

- What are some things you can do to get unstuck? What do you need to surrender to God to move forward? Share what you've discovered with a trusted friend, family member, or counselor, and ask that person to hold you accountable for growth in this area.

FIVE

NO LONGER IN EDEN

The Christian does not think God will love us because we are good, but that God will make us good because He loves us.

—C. S. Lewis

S ometimes even wise people end up in a mess. Too often, recovering idiots like me find themselves in a stinky pile of something far worse. The unfortunate reality is that we *all* fail.

We all cheat.

We all lie.

We all pretend.

We all say one thing and do another.

We all sin.

All of us.

It's not all the time, and we might even go for an hour or two without sinning, but something always betrays our new and true identity in Christ. And we blow it every stinkin' day.

A thought.

A look.

A word.

Something stupid that misses the mark of perfection.

At the risk of sounding cynical and fatalistic, let's own it: Sin is in our DNA. We are fallen human beings who have a bent toward the dark side of our nature.

Yes, I know, we are new creatures in Christ.[34] Of course, those who belong to Christ are redeemed and have a new identity in Jesus. Paul makes it clear that we are delivered from our wretchedness and we are no longer slaves to sin.[35] But none of us is perfect, and we're no longer naked in Eden. In truth, we're all hiding, still trying to cover our shame rather than own it.

More than I'd like to admit, I wrestle sometimes with lust. Temptation is *not* a sin, but to linger with a lustful thought is crossing a line—a line I flirt with at times. I'm happily married to a beautiful wife, but an unholy desire for something or someone else still happens occasionally.

James, the brother of Jesus, once wrote, "Each person's own desires and thoughts . . . drag them into evil and lure them away into darkness."[36] Yep. Been there. And it's alarming how close we all are to one bad decision that can ruin everything.

Fact check: We're human. Which means, on this side of eternity, you and I will always struggle with our old nature that is nothing like our new nature in Jesus.

As a Christ follower, and because of what Jesus did on the cross, I don't live bound by sin or trapped in hopelessness. I am perfect in my position before God. However, I am still far from perfect in my practice and day-to-day experience. I have a long way to grow—and so do you.

Yes, relationally, we're in a new Eden now—in a perfect interpersonal place with God because of Jesus but still hiding at times and painfully aware of our imperfections.

---

34 2 Corinthians 5:17.

35 See Romans 7.

36 James 1:14 (TPT).

So, what should we do? How should we live? Well, here's a radical idea: Stop hiding. If we all still sin (and we all do), then why wouldn't we just step out of the darkness, own it, and confess our brokenness to one another? Why hide in the shadows feeling hopeless when we can live free in the light? James said that confession is the path to healing.[37]

A WISE GUY, BUT . . .

The story of King Solomon has always fascinated me. It is an epic saga of intrigue, survival, blessing, and tragic failure.

Solomon was blessed by God and had no equal. In 1 Kings 3:13, God promised him both wealth and honor. He was wise and intelligent. In 1 Kings 4:29 (NIV), the Bible says God gave Solomon "wisdom and very great insight, and a breadth of understanding as measureless as the sand on the seashore."

Solomon must have had a giant "S" under his royal robe. This guy was the Superman of rulers in his day. Apparently, his sexual appetite was unequaled as well, and that led to some foolish mistakes—about one thousand of them (seven hundred wives and three hundred concubines).

Sadly, by the time we get to his story in 1 Kings 11:1–2 (NIV), everything starts to unravel. We are told that the king "loved many foreign women . . . from nations about which the LORD had told the Israelites, 'You must not intermarry with them, because they will sure-ly turn your hearts after other gods.' Nevertheless, Solomon held fast to them in love." And sure enough, his seven hundred wives and three hundred concubines led him astray. (For the record, I don't blame the women; I blame the man. Solomon was responsible for his poor choices.)

Perhaps the saddest line in his story is found in 1 Kings 11:4: "As Solomon grew old, his wives turned his heart after other gods, and his heart was not fully devoted to the LORD his God."

---

37 James 5:16.

The result? He lost the kingdom of his father David. "So the LORD said to Solomon, 'Since this is your attitude and you have not kept my covenant and my decrees, which I commanded you, I will most certainly tear the kingdom away from you and give it to one of your subordinates.'"[38]

Talk about a tragic tale of agony and loss. Why did this guy start so well but end so badly? How can you go from being the wisest of the wise to the guy who is sacrificing offerings to false gods?

A FEW OF SOLOMON'S PROBLEMS

First, he chose to put his desires above God's command to avoid ungodly women. It's true: Bad company corrupts good morals.[39] When we choose our way over God's way, it always leads us astray.

Solomon's life of sexual self-indulgence, with his hundreds of wives and concubines, led to unrestraint in his spiritual life. When we refuse to practice self-control in one area, our lack of discipline often leads to foolishness in others.

Solomon also demonstrated how affluence often leads to spiritual laziness. I'm not saying rich people are always spiritually apathetic, but Jesus said it's tough for the rich to enter the kingdom of God.[40] Why? Because there are too many distractions.

On the other hand, I know from personal experience that poverty leads to desperation and desperation leads to prayer! And prayer keeps us focused on the Father.

The pride of Solomon led to his downfall. Arrogance frequently leads to decadence—especially when we think we know more than anyone else, including God. It's entirely possible that this king started to believe his own press ("I'm great, I'm wise!"). I can't help but shake

---

38   1 Kings 11:11.

39   1 Corinthians 15:33.

40   Mark 10:25.

my head at the irony. Here's what he wrote earlier in his life: "Pride goes before destruction, a haughty spirit before a fall."[41]

In his later years, King Solomon had multiple adversaries and, even worse, he had a heart that was cold and distant from God. His disastrous ending was a far cry from his glorious beginning.

On a regular basis, I pray, "God, help me to finish well." I don't expect to live without imperfections. I know I will make plenty of mistakes along the way. But I want to stay faithful to the end.

By the way, Solomon's dad, David, failed at times too. The difference between father and son? David relented and repented.[42] Solomon didn't.

At any point, if Solomon had owned his failure and turned back to the Lord, God would have redeemed, restored, and renewed him. It is what God does best, and that's why I plan on being an incredibly good repenter to the very end.

HOW WE GET THERE

Most of us do not leap into devastating sin; we crawl into it bit by bit. In fact, it's relatively rare to stumble into a significant failure by accident or in one giant explosion of idiocy. A major compromise almost always is the result of many minor compromises made along the way.

Sadly, I know this from firsthand experience. As I confessed earlier, my past is littered with a thousand examples of what *not* to do. I'm not saying this to gain your pity. I'm not trying to be self-deprecating, either. Neither am I throwing up my hands in defeat and surrendering to my humanness. I will and must continue to grow and be molded into the image of Jesus. (Christians call this the process of *sanctification*.)

But if sin is defined as missing the mark through words, actions, or thoughts, then I fail on a regular basis. If sin is knowing what good

41 Proverbs 16:18 (NIV).

42 See Psalm 51.

I am to do and yet not doing it, then I have blown it many, many times.[43]

Someone once asked me, "How do I know—really know—if I'm sinning?"

Here are my simple answers:

- If you don't want to tell anyone and you want to keep it a secret, then it is probably a sin.

- If you are investing an extraordinary amount of time and energy trying to rationalize or justify your actions, then it is probably a sin.

- If something you've done has you bound in fear—such as the fear of getting caught or exposed—then it's definitely a sin.

- If the Word says it's a sin, it's a sin.

In my experience, every time I forget who I am, Whom I belong to, and what God has done for me, then I begin to descend into darkness.

Every time.

James also made it clear that our failures are the result of one poor choice made after another. He said, "Each person is tempted when they are dragged away by their own evil desire and enticed. Then, after desire has conceived, it gives birth to sin; and sin, when it is full-grown, gives birth to death."[44] Lots of poor decisions are made along the path to devastation and death.

Again, we all fail. Often. And that can lead to some horrible despair and hopelessness. By God's grace and the work of the Holy Spirit, we should sin less than we used to, but it's still more than we want to or should. That's the bad news, but good news follows: If we

---

43 James 4:17.

44 James 1:14–15 (NIV).

own our sin and confess it to God, the Lord is faithful and always ready to forgive us.

God knows us better than we know ourselves, but absolutely nothing we do will make Him love us any more (or any less!) than He already does.

Sin consumes us with guilt, shame, and fear, but God's specialty is restoration. That's why David prayed, "Restore to me the joy of your salvation."[45] He knew God could restore him. God promises us that He will sweep away our sin like morning mist. He says His mercies toward us are inexhaustible (i.e., they're new every morning).[46]

Does this mean that what we do doesn't truly matter all that much? Of course not. (Paul addressed this in Romans 6.) You and I need to grow. Without question, we need to learn to walk in holiness. Yet God forgives. He is good, merciful, kind, and gracious. He knows that we are but dust and still a work in progress.[47]

Though you and I are new, redeemed, and perfect in our *position* in Christ, it's our *practice* of godliness that is still a work in progress.

That being said, let's consider some of the reasons why we fail.

HEART CHECK

Here are eight reasons why we blow it:

- We want to sin because the pleasure is hard to resist. Even though the spirit is willing, the flesh is weak.

- We've developed bad habits that need to be unlearned.

- We fail to have accountability partners who will ask us hard questions.

---

45 Psalm 51:12 (NIV).

46 Isaiah 44:22; Lamentations 3:22–23.

47 Psalm 103:14.

- We fail to recognize that we are in the middle of a spiritual battle with evil.

- We have not learned to identify the triggers that trip us.

- We do not practice walking in the fullness and power of the Holy Spirit—daily.

- We are not practicing spiritual disciplines that help us put off the old person and put on the new.

- We react out of our pain from our past or present experiences that upset us rather than respond in a holy way that honors God.

If you're failing more than not, it's time to evaluate why. Being honest about the reason (or reasons) is the only way to grow and keep moving forward. Failure does not have to be fatal.

So drop the arrogance and pride. Own your humanness but embrace grace and learn from your failures. You are a work in progress, and progress is what matters most. By the way, you can have hope in Christ because the Word promises that what Jesus has started in you, He will finish.[48]

THAT'S GOTTA BE EMBARRASSING!

A woman caught in adultery was dragged before Jesus by men ready to stone her to death.[49] She was embarrassed, ashamed, and afraid for her life. Her encounter with Jesus, however, was another example of the mercy of God. Jesus didn't condemn her, but He said, "Go now and leave your life of sin."[50]

Jesus loved, accepted, and forgave this woman, and then He

---

48 Philippians 1:6.

49 See the story in John 8.

50 John 8:11 (NIV).

challenged her to change and to grow. That is the way of Jesus and the path He calls us to follow.

When we fail—and we will—we must remember that God is bigger than our mistakes. And because He can restore, renew, and redeem any life surrendered to Him, our sin does not have to be the end of our story. Our failures and weaknesses are never beyond God's faithfulness. Shameless desperation is that moment when you realize your desperation never ends in despair when God is in the mix.

That's good news. Very good news for all of us, and the reason I'm still thankful for God's amazing and epic grace.

So, my friend, whatever you've done, always run *to* God, not *from* Him.[51]

He's got this.

He's got you.

You are never hopeless when the God of hope is involved.

---

51 Hebrews 4:14–16.

A GRACE REFLECTION (A POEM)

A thousand times I've come to Him
A thousand times undone
A thousand times He's rescued me
And now a thousand one
What is this love
That holds me close
Regardless of my sin
What is this hope
A grace defined
Completely found in Him
A thousand times He's come to me
A thousand times redone
A thousand times I'm found in Him
And now a thousand one[52]

---

52 A poem I wrote and posted on my blog, kurtbubna.com, February 2015.

EPIC STEPS

- Review the list in this chapter regarding how to know if you're sinning. Is there something you don't want to look at or talk about? If so, why? You're at a crossroads right now. You can choose to confess it and get free—or not. What are you going to do?

- Look again at the "heart check" list. What one or two things might be the reason why you're failing in a particular area? Evaluate the reason(s) why. Ask God to change your heart and your mind. Ask someone you love and trust to help you.

SIX

THIRTY-ONE MILLION SECONDS

Jesus is a dream restorer.
—*Louie Giglio*

Thirty-one million seconds sounds like a lot of time, but it's not. And it's all you have in any given year to live and make a difference. Before you know it, millions of moments are gone forever.

At some point, the wrinkled face looking back at you in the mirror with its wear and tear might surprise you. It may feel like you're looking at the "ghost of Christmas future" and you're haunted with a prospect that scares you. You wonder, *Have I used my time and gifts wisely?*

I've lived for almost two billion seconds (you do the math), and I've decided I don't want to squander one more moment on *anything* that's meaningless or empty. Life is too short to waste.

I had a dear friend, Taylor, who was once the epitome of beauty. Young, slim, with dark hair and eyes, and a smile that seemed both enchanting and a little mischievous. At only twenty-nine, she had accomplished so much that she was the envy of her coworkers and friends. It seemed to all who knew her that she was destined for greatness. Then came the diagnosis that changed everything. "You have stage four cervical cancer." Within a year, she was gone.

Scott was an active outdoorsman and chiseled like a Greek god. For years, he held numerous sports records at his alma mater. As an adult, he always exercised and ate well, and he was famous for his strict avoidance of germs and sick people. Despite his best efforts, however, Scott passed away at the not-so-ripe age of thirty-eight after a long battle with colon cancer.

Thirty-one million seconds are priceless, especially when there's no guarantee you own the next one. Taylor and Scott are still remembered for a lot of things, but most of all, I remember them for the utter surprise I faced when they died. Apparently, life *really is* short—much shorter than some of us realize.

Most of my life, I've lived aware that we all have an expiration date. Being exposed to death at an early age made me prematurely aware of my mortality. I was seven or eight when a classmate in school died of leukemia. Of course, I had no idea what leukemia was or why it took the life of my friend, but I do remember thinking, *Someday, I will probably die of something. I just hope it doesn't hurt.*

Forgive me if this all seems a bit morbid. My intent is not to scare or depress you. (This is a book about hope!) I certainly don't want anyone to fixate on death. However, it is my deep conviction that when you are aware of your limited time on *terra firma*, then you will live the kind of passionate, intentional, and hope-filled life God intended for you to live.

Don't live in fear of the inevitable (i.e., death), but in the meantime, don't waste the gifts you have, especially the gift of time.

Jesus knew His season walking this earth was limited, and that fact drove Him to make the best use of His time. He wasn't driven by the tyranny of the urgent, but He was compelled to accomplish His God-given assignment. He told the twelve, "As long as it is day, we must do the works of him who sent me. Night is coming, when no one can work."[53]

---

53 John 9:4 (NIV).

I AM A CANCER SURVIVOR

I've written elsewhere about my battle with cancer, but it still seems odd to me to read those words: *cancer survivor*. Even though my dad died of cancer, as well as too many other family members and friends, it wasn't until I heard from my doctor "I'm afraid we're dealing with cancer" that I *ever* thought about it happening to me. Denial and I are tight.

Sadly, according to the World Health Organization (WHO), cancer is the second leading cause of death, causing millions of deaths globally every year.[54] That's a disturbing statistic, but even more so when it's personal, and it *is* very personal for some. You would be hard-pressed to find anyone who hasn't had someone they know and love die of cancer.

At fifty-four, and relatively healthy, I went for my annual physical. Every year, the worst part of the exam came when the doctor checked my prostate. Typically, and thankfully, this was a quick part of my examination. Usually, as he pulled off his rubber glove, I'd hear something from the doc like, "Looks good. All is well." Of course, I never felt very well after *that* experience, but I was always relieved to get a good report.

That year was different, and my doc wasn't that quick, and what he said was more than a little disturbing. "Hmmm, I'm going to wait to see what your PSA levels are, but I might need to send you to a urologist."

Have you ever been to see a urologist? Don't misunderstand me— I'm thankful for all doctors and realize that each has a vital medical role to play. But seriously, why would anyone want to practice urology or proctology?

Sure enough, about a week or so later, I got a postcard in the mail from my general practitioner asking me to make a follow-up visit to

---

54 World Health Organization, "Cancer: Key Facts," September 12, 2018, https://www.who.int/news-room/fact-sheets/detail/cancer.

discuss my PSA levels. I had a sick feeling in my gut that this was not going to be fun, and it wasn't.

My regular family doctor is a Christian and a great guy. Except for the fact that he's a vegetarian, I think he's fantastic. But when he referred me to the dreaded urology specialist, I wasn't too happy. Of course, I asked him a few questions about prostate cancer, and he merely said, "Let's not get ahead of ourselves. It's best we take this one step at a time. The guy who messes with prostates for a living and charges twice as much as me is better able to answer all your questions." (He might not have said exactly that last part.)

Not jumping to fearful conclusions is wise counsel unless you're freaking out and wondering if there's cancer in your body. That night, while I was trying to go to sleep, my self-talk was relentless . . .

If I do have cancer, how is this going to change my life?

Why is this happening? I knew all that pizza was going to kill me!

What if this is it . . . the end of the line . . . the last dance . . . the grand finale? (I can be a bit melodramatic at times; at least that's what my wife says.)

I tossed and turned for over an hour until I finally decided that if I was awake, I might as well pray. And pray I did. I got out of bed, and in the darkness of my living room, I knelt at the couch and cried out, "God, I know asking *why* is not as important as asking *what*. So, *what* do you want me to do? What are you trying to show me through all this? What the heck is going on?" (Yes, I know, the last question is pretty much a disguised *why* question.)

Unless you've experienced God's presence during a great trial—and I hope you have—it's difficult to explain how His peace can invade your panic. I didn't have any visions. The heavens didn't part. There was no handwriting on the wall, and no audible voice. However, I did hear God speak to my heart, and He said what I needed to hear: "Kurt, you ain't dead yet!"

I will admit to you that I was tempted to explore precisely what God meant by "yet," but I understood God's challenge. It was an encouragement to stop worrying about the inevitable (i.e., we all eventually die of something) and to make sure that I lived all 86,400 seconds of each remaining day with intentionality and purpose.

ON CRUISE CONTROL

Honestly, for at least a few years prior to my cancer, I'd pretty much been living life on cruise control. Routine and risk avoidance had become the norm for me. I hadn't quit on life; I just wasn't as fully engaged as I had been on most of my days before turning fifty.

By fifty, I'd experienced a measure of success. Capable people surrounded me at work and didn't need or require micromanaging. I had a beautiful home in a friendly neighborhood with nice neighbors. I'd been all over the world. There wasn't much, if anything, left on my bucket list. Life was good. So, I hit the cruise button, sat back, and relaxed.

When God responded to my heart's cry with "You ain't dead yet!" it was like a shot of adrenaline injected into my heart. And at that moment, I saw how comfortable I'd grown and realized again that a path of ease can be a great enemy to a life of radical, hope-infused faith.

One of my oldest friends was a man named Noel Campbell. He went to be with Jesus some time ago, but he was a mentor and pastor to me for a very long time. In his fifties, Noel used to kick my twentysomething butt on the racquetball court on a regular basis. He was always very fit and physically active. In fact, the only time I ever beat him was the time he *let* me beat him out of pity.

At the end of his life, Noel had limited physical capability, but his mind was still sharp and his heart still full of godly wisdom. For over thirty-five years, I'd watched Noel model a life of faith. He was famous among his friends for saying *yes* to Jesus no matter the personal cost or sacrifice. By the world's standards, he had very little, but in the kingdom of God, Noel was a hero to many. Noel would say, "Follow

Jesus. Always. No matter what. Because you're never too old for God to use you."

Some of you are young, and you're finding it hard to relate. For you, life is fresh and new and exciting. You're convinced that something remarkable is around the next corner. I applaud your zest for living. Hold on to that passion for life but trust me on this: things change. Life can wear you down, and we are all at risk of letting our days become little more than a boring routine. We all tend to drift toward getting stuck in our comfort zones.

Others are a bit perturbed with me right now. You like your comfortable, La-Z-Boy life. The closest thing you know of adventure is watching reality TV. You may not say it out loud, but you often think, *I'll leave any bold undertaking to the young.*

Of course, you've got reasonable excuses:

I'm too old.

I've got too many responsibilities.

I have health issues.

I've worked hard for what I have . . . it's time to chill on a beach somewhere.

At my age, you must be careful; risk-taking can kill ya!

Perhaps, however, something is stirring in your soul. Maybe there is a growing realization in your mind of this truth: God's *not* finished with you, either.

Some old fogies are fond of saying, "Youth is wasted on the young!" But hopefully, it's beginning to dawn on you: You're never too old (or too young) for God to use you. In fact, age isn't a liability; it's an asset.

Here's a little thought-provoking insight: We all have the same amount of time. Regardless of your age, the thirty-one million seconds in a year are the same for everybody. I know it seems like time passes more quickly with age, but it doesn't. Maybe it just feels faster because you waste more time in your self-made rut of boredom. Maybe yesterday looks a lot like today because it is, so the days blend like white noise in your soul, without any notable moments of adventure. You've forgotten how to dance to the music of life because it's easier not to dance.

Do you remember Susan Boyle? This Scottish singer became an overnight sensation when she stepped onto a stage and sang like an angel. Did you know she was forty-eight when she first appeared on *Britain's Got Talent* in 2009?

Jessica Tandy (star of *Driving Miss Daisy;* Google it if you're under forty) was eighty years old when she won an Academy Award for best actress.

Monet was still painting with passion and skill when he was in his seventies and eighties, and Picasso was still active at ninety.

Former Beatles superstar, Paul McCartney, was still actively performing in his seventies.

Abraham was seventy-five when God promised him a son (a scary thought for any empty-nester).

And my personal favorite, C. S. Lewis, undeniably one of the greatest Christian writers of the twentieth century, wrote in his fifties *The Chronicles of Narnia* (which has sold over one hundred million copies in forty-one languages).[55]

Age can be an asset. Experience can provide a wealth of knowledge and wisdom. So, whatever your age, the big question is: Are you living with purpose and intentionality?

If you're breathing, you ain't dead yet!

Facing the unknown of cancer was a much needed wake-up call for me. It jarred me from complacency. It shook me to my core. But through it all, God reminded me that He wasn't finished with me yet.

I went back to bed after that moment of revelation in my living room and slept soundly. I woke up the next morning, and every morning since then, thanking God for another day to follow Him. Thanking Him for another opportunity to grow. Grateful for another daily chunk of those thirty-one million seconds to make a difference.

---

55 Wikipedia, s.v. "C. S. Lewis," last edited September 17, 2019, http://
    en.wikipedia.org/wiki/C._S._Lewis.

PERSPECTIVE MATTERS

Let me suggest a few simple ways you can have your moment of revelation without facing a life-threatening disease as I did.

First, step back and get a different perspective. Embrace the view that includes your life many years after you are gone, but live like you can make a difference now—because you can.

If you're twentysomething and you think that *old* automatically means *outdated* and *useless*, then change your point of view. Someone once said, "It's not how old you are. It's how you are old that matters."[56]

Second, create a spiritual bucket list.[57] Whether you are young or not so young, an essential part of living on purpose is having some bold spiritual goals and a plan to accomplish them. Too many people wander through life without any idea of what they might achieve if they only put their mind to it.

My late uncle, pastor, and author, Don Bubna, was a stellar example of living on purpose. He stayed active well into his eighties. He once asked me, "Nephew, what would you attempt for God if you knew you could not fail?" Of course, I thought, *But we do fail, and sometimes miserably!* However, my uncle's point was profound: Live big because we have a great big God, and if you don't aim high, it's probably because your view of God is too small.

A spiritual bucket list is a list of things you'd love to do for God before you die. It might include something as simple as finally reading through the entire Bible. It might involve telling your best friend about Jesus before it's too late. It might be writing a book of your precious memories and lessons learned for your children and your children's

---

56 Ownership of this quote is disputed. It is often attributed to French author Jules Renard, but no sound source is yet found for this attribution. There is a possibility that it may have been said or written in French by Renard. The earliest source found for this quote in English is in the mid-1900s, and all the sources attributed this quote to Marie Dressler.

57 The idea of a "bucket list" became well-known through the movie *The Bucket List* starring Jack Nicholson and Morgan Freeman. Essentially, it is a list of things you wish to do before you die (or kick the bucket).

children. (Who cares if it gets traditionally published? Write it for your family.) It could be serving as a volunteer chaplain in a hospital or using some of your nest egg to go on a mission trip to China. My friend Noel Campbell learned to play the violin in his seventies, and it became an instrument of worship for him.

Take a moment right now and pray, "God, what would you like me to do with the rest of my life—more specifically, with the next thirty-one million seconds I have on earth?"

The final thing you must do, and this is critical, is to pick something and pull the trigger. Get in the game. If you're young, don't wait to do something great, someday. If you're old, don't be like so many others who think life has passed them by. It's time to stop making excuses and go for it.

God is not finished with you.

KARATE, COUNTRY MUSIC, DRUMS, AND JESUS

There is a middle-aged guy in our church who consistently surprises me. His name is Jesse, and he happens to have Down syndrome.

I have no idea what Jesse's IQ is, but it's not very high. He's functional but childlike, and he always has and always will live with his mom. Anybody who knows Jesse knows he's passionate about four things: karate, country music, drums, and Jesus. I don't think I've ever seen him without a cowboy hat or a T-shirt displaying his favorite country western musician, and he has often been seen playing air drums during worship in church.

Week after week, Jesse shows up early to get a front-row seat right next to me in our church auditorium. (He doesn't understand that most people prefer the back seats.) He sits up front near me because he enjoys being close to the action and the drums in the worship band. More than many churchgoers, Jesse engages with all of his heart in worship. His love for Jesus is both evident and humbling.

One Sunday morning during a worship song that deeply touched me, I ended up on my knees singing, crying, and quietly praying. I'm sure several of those around me noticed, but I didn't care. I was lost in the presence of Jesus.

My eyes were closed and my arms were lifted up when a small hand on my shoulder startled me. I opened my eyes to see who had the nerve to interrupt me. It was Jesse; his eyelids were squeezed shut, and he was praying for me. To say I became a blubbering, sobbing mess at that point would be an understatement. In no time, I was on my face sucking carpet. What I saw first as an interruption became one of the most powerful spiritual moments of my life. Somehow, I knew Jesus was touching and blessing me through my friend Jesse.

What does Jesse have to do with living a life of hope and intentionality? What can you and I learn from him? A lot, but this particular lesson is clear and straightforward. Few of us suffer from any debilitating handicap. Most of us are quite capable of doing whatever we want to do whenever we want to do it. But too often, we hold back in fear or check out in apathy rather than jump in with faith, hope, and enthusiasm.

We need to be more like Jesse. We need to function with the clear and simple focus of wholehearted devotion to God. We need to pursue the Father and His plans with passionate abandonment. We need to worry less about what others think. And we must learn to live with a determined and deliberate desire to discover all that our Creator has fashioned for us to do in Him.

If Jesse can do it, so can we.

MAKE IT COUNT

Most of my life, I've shown up early to everything. In my opinion, if you're not early, you're late. On the other hand, being late to my grave is just fine with me. In the meantime, I hope to make every day and every moment I have count for something way bigger than me, something eternal.

The only thing that separates life from death is one heartbeat and one second, but there's a whole world of difference between living and dying, so choose well and live well.

Live life on purpose.

Live with passion.

Live with a commitment to make every one of those thirty-one million seconds—and beyond—count for something eternal.

Make the best use of your time despite life's challenges.[58] That, my friend, is living and walking in the epic life of uncommon hope. If you don't, you'll lose far more than time.

---

58 Ephesians 5:16.

EPIC STEPS

- Think back over the last twenty-four hours of your life. Did you treat every moment as a priceless gift from God? If not, why?

- What was the last thing to happen in your life that was a wake-up call reminding you of your mortality? How can that moment jar you from any apathy or from living on cruise control?

- Take some time to dream, think, and pray about your spiritual bucket list. (Remember, it's a list of things you want to do for God before you die.) Once you have a list, pick one thing and pull the trigger soon (like, this week).

SEVEN

DOES MY LIFE MATTER?

My mission in life is not merely to survive, but to thrive and to do so with some passion, some compassion, some humor, and some style.

—*Maya Angelou*

When you come to your very last day on this side of eternity, what do you want your friends and family to remember about you? In other words, what do you want people to say about your life? And perhaps more importantly, how do *you* want to feel about your time on planet Earth?

Here's the thing about dying: Everybody experiences death eventually.

More than once, I've been at the bed of someone who is near death. If they are Christ followers, it's not depressing, but it's always sobering. I was with an elderly man named David just a few days before he passed. I will never forget when he looked me in the eye (in a moment of unusual clarity for someone on pain meds), and he asked, "Pastor Kurt, have I made a difference, and did my life truly matter?" That question is important to most of us. I reminded David of his three kids and thirteen grandkids who adore him, and the many others in his life he profoundly impacted.

Some people face the end of their lives with deep satisfaction and few regrets. Others finish poorly with questions about what might have been.

Here's what I know deep in my knower: God wants you to finish well, and critical to doing so is discovering your God-given purpose. Rick Warren wrote in his book, *The Purpose Driven Life*, "The greatest tragedy is not death, but life without purpose."

I believe that truth with all my heart, but right now, what I think doesn't matter as much as what you believe. So, before I give you some ideas about how to discover your God-given purpose and how that brings great hope to your life, let's consider why it's important to do so.

WHY GOD WANTS YOU TO KNOW YOUR PURPOSE

A young woman I call Suzy came to me some time ago, and in frustration, she said, "Everybody has a plan for my life but me! I have no idea who I am, why I'm here, or what my purpose is. And I'm pretty sure I've screwed things up too bad to be used by God for anything meaningful."

Suzy was a single mom with a record and a history of substance abuse. She did about a year in jail for a drug-related charge, and the only job she could get was working for a local burger joint earning minimum wage. The look on her face and the desperation in her voice are things I've seen too often. Most everyone with a history of failure tends to struggle with self-worth.

I told Suzy what I'm telling you: Every life matters, and God has a destiny for all of us no matter what we've done. Unfortunately, many people focus on their past and are quick (too quick) to disqualify themselves from any meaningful future. Over the years, I have had the privilege of telling thousands, "The boundaries of your past never have to be the horizons of your future." God doesn't ignore your past, but if you surrender your life to Him and to His power to redeem, restore, and renew, He shapes your past and your pain into a masterful work of art. He makes something beautiful out of garbage.

Here's the first reason why discovering your purpose matters: You are the only you there is. No one else on the planet now, a thousand years ago, or a thousand years from now is like you. God didn't just break the mold after creating you; there never was a mold in the first place. More than you probably realize, you have a unique place and purpose on this planet.

Think about it. If I am the only Kurt Bubna who will ever live in all of time on this planet with the experiences and gifts that I have, then that has to mean something. If you are the only you who will ever be in all of history, then you matter to God, to others, and to you.

We hear it all the time: "There's nobody like you!" Sadly, however, sometimes we either don't understand what that means, or we forget the implications of that truth. You matter. God never does anything by accident. Your parents may or may not have planned your birth, but God still has a plan for your life! And He created you the way you are for a purpose that has eternal ramifications.

The apostle Paul wrote to the church in Ephesus, "For we are God's masterpiece. He has created us anew in Christ Jesus, so that we can do the good things he planned for us long ago."[59] God is a skilled architect with a master plan for each and every one of us, and that's why discovering your purpose truly matters.

Here's the second reason why this is important: Without awareness and acceptance of your purpose, you will be distracted by the worthless idols of our culture and wander. In fact, knowing your God-given purpose is like a compass in your life that helps you stay on course. It gives direction. It helps determine what you will do and what you won't do with your time, energy, money, and talents. If,

---

59 Ephesians 2:10 (NLT).

and when, you know what you're all about and what your God-given purpose is, that understanding helps you know what to say *yes* to and what to say *no* to in life.

In many ways, your choices and decisions are simplified when you know your purpose. For example, let's say a part of your God-given purpose is to be a parent who invests in the lives of your kids for the kingdom of God. Being a godly parent is probably not your only purpose, but when you see the value and implications of that purpose, your decisions about time, energy, money, and talents will always be filtered through that understanding. And knowing your parental purpose to raise kids who love God simplifies the choices and decisions you make as a family about what *is* and *isn't* essential. Knowing your purpose, whatever it is, helps you get where you need to be and helps remove distractions and confusion by simplifying everything.

Here's one more reason why God wants you to know your purpose: It's the best pathway to lasting and meaningful joy. The need for happiness highly motivates humans. If the history of the human race has one common thread, it's that we live for the pursuit of happiness. We long for joy. We look for fun. We search for pleasure. In fact, the hunt for bliss drives us and motivates us like nothing else.

Let me be clear about something: There is a potential holy side to our longings. There is a God-created part of our human psyche that rightfully longs for joy. The problem is that we all too often end up looking for joy in all the wrong places. We attempt to fill that longing in our soul through way too many things that are a far cry from what God wants for us and from how He intended for that longing to be met.

Some time ago, there was an article by Warren Buffet in *Parade Magazine*. It was called "10 Ways to Get Rich."[60] Warren Buffet is considered to be the richest man in the world with an estimated fortune of well over $60 billion. In the article, he gives ten principles he

---

60 Joel Brown, Addicted2Success, "Do It Like Warren Buffett: 10 Ways to Get Rich," published April 21, 2011, https://addicted2success.com/success-advice/10-ways-to-get-rich/.

used to go from two cents to billions of dollars. And to his credit, his tenth principle is to "know what success really means." Buffet defines success not by how much money you have, but by how many people truly love you. He offers this interesting insight: "I know people who have a lot of money and they get testimonial dinners and hospital wings named after them. But the truth is that nobody in the world loves them."

You see, money is not the key to happiness, and having lots of stuff is not the key to true and lasting joy. I have a friend who is filthy rich, but he's on his third marriage, his kids despise him, and he lives on Rolaids and Valium! Obviously, that's not happiness, that's not joy, and that's not God's plan or idea. His plan is that we find Him and His purpose for our lives.

HOW TO KNOW YOUR PURPOSE

Okay, let's shift gears and take a look at how to discover your God-given purpose.

First, ask God. (Did you just sigh?) I know it's probably a no-brainer, but if you want to know what God's purpose and plan are for your life, it starts with going to the Source and asking Him.

Here's what Jesus said: "Ask and it will be given to you; seek and you will find; knock and the door will be opened to you."[61] In context, Jesus is talking about prayer here. However, the principle we can hang our hat on in this verse is that God answers when we ask. (Though *how* He answers sometimes surprises us, but that's another story.) The point here is that God's not playing hide-and-seek with us; He wants us to know what we need to know.

Frank came to me after I spoke at our church about discovering our purpose. He was mad. He said, "For far too long, I have searched for my purpose. I've asked God over and over what His plan is for me,

---

61 Matthew 7:7 (NIV).

and He's not answering me!" Frank felt God was elusive or perhaps overlooking him.

Maybe you've struggled here too.

Something in your soul knows you were created for a purpose. You're desperate to see at least a basic blueprint for your life. You've read Jeremiah 29:11 a gazillion times: "I know the plans I have for you, declares the LORD . . ." but now you want to scream and kick the dog every time someone quotes that verse to you.

So, at this point, you've decided that God is ignoring you, you're not worthy of a holy purpose, there is no plan, or there is no God. Cluelessness leads to hopelessness. I know. But let me give you a couple of other things worth doing before you give up.

Here's the second step to discovering your purpose: Ask yourself. What stirs your heart? What gets you all excited and pumped up? Unless it's something obviously unholy (like becoming a serial killer), then it's quite possible that God put that passion in your heart. Someone once said, "Life isn't measured by the number of breaths we take, but by the moments that take our breath away."

When I coached track, one of the assistants was a guy who ran for the University of Oregon. He told me once that he wasn't sure if God could use him at the university. His mother wanted him to go to Bible school to become a pastor. I told him that the last thing God wanted was for everyone to become preachers!

He loved to run. He said he was born to run. So I told him to run! Run for God, run to bring Him pleasure, and run to put a smile on God's face.

The psalmist wrote, "My heart is stirred by a noble theme."[62] Sometimes it is as simple as considering where your heart is stirred. Where do you most feel God's pleasure? What are your natural and supernatural gifts and passions? A huge part of determining God's plan for your life is recognizing what excites and motivates you. Don't over-

---

62 Psalm 45:1 (NIV).

look, discount, or minimize what's in you. It may be a God-deposit put there for an eternal purpose.

There's one more important part in the discovery process: Ask others. Put a different way, what do your friends and family have to say? What do the people closest to you who know you best and love you the most think? I'm not saying that your mom or your BFF is always right. You'll go looney tunes trying to listen to everybody who has the "perfect plan" for your life. I'm also not suggesting that we live to please others. That never ends well because we are to please God, but others can be a confirming voice in your life. The input of a faithful friend should sound like an echo in your soul; it's something you've already heard from God and your own heart.

The wisest guy to ever walk the planet, Solomon, once wrote, "Plans fail for lack of counsel, but with many advisers they succeed."[63] It's okay—and wise, in fact—to get the advice of trusted voices in your life.

Ask the people around you these questions:

- What do you think are my greatest strengths?

- What do you believe is my greatest passion?

- When you look at my life, where do you see me making the greatest impact?

- What should I stop or start doing?

Then listen and listen well. God wants you to know His plan for your life more than you can imagine.

YOU'VE GOT TO BE KIDDING

A long time ago, back when dinosaurs still roamed the earth, I was in college and wanted to become a fireman. Driving fast (legally) and

---

63 Proverbs 15:22 (NIV).

saving lives seemed like a good career choice for me. I've always been a bit of an adrenaline junkie.

Then one morning at breakfast, a friend asked me whether I'd ever thought about going to Bible school to become a pastor. I almost laughed out loud as I choked on my bagel. "You've got to be kidding me," I said. "No way!"

I told my dear wife, Laura, what my friend had said. I was hoping she would laugh it off with me. I was counting on her to affirm the ridiculousness of the idea of me as a preacher. To my utter dismay, she said, "Well, the Lord told me I would be a pastor's wife someday." (My first thought was, *I wonder who she's going to marry after me?*)

A few more days passed. Then one morning during my devotions, I read a passage in Jeremiah.[64] While reading God's call to Jerry, God called me. I can hardly describe how powerfully this text hit me. It was as if God had ripped these words out of time and history and had spoken them just to me. He also spoke to my heart that day: "You can do anything you want to do, and I will bless and use you, but you were made to serve me as a pastor." I had a moment of revelation that changed me and redirected the course of my life.

I knew I could be a fireman and a paramedic and serve God, but I also knew that good is not always best. And God's best for me was to be a pastor.

For the record, I'm not saying that being a pastor is better than being a fireman, or that pastors are more important than firefighters. So please don't think you have to become a missionary or a minister to be in your God-ordained sweet spot. Going into full-time Christian service doesn't require working for a church. You can and should serve God wherever you work and in whatever you do. But starting that day, something began to change in my heart.

God spoke. My friends, my pastor, and my wife confirmed my call. And deep in my soul, I knew God had been preparing me my

---

64 Jeremiah 1:4–10.

entire life to be a pastor. The result? Pastoring became the desire of my heart. Go figure.

No matter what God has planned for you, the key to discovering His plan is to *ask*.

Ask God.

Ask yourself.

Ask your friends.

It's simple. Not always easy, but not as complicated as we sometimes make it, either.

So, speaking of asking, let me ask one more question: What are you doing to discover and embrace God's dream and purpose for you?

You may have lost hope. You may have given up on yourself or on God. But you have a destiny. You have a God-given purpose and your life matters. A lot.

Remember my friend, Suzy, the single mom with a broken past? Well, she finally began to believe God had a plan for her, and today she's working with other recovering addicts and single moms as an instrument of uncommon hope for others.

Ain't God good?

EPIC STEPS

- Do you have a fairly good idea of your God-given purpose? If so, can you state it in one or two sentences?

- If you're not sure of your purpose, go back and read again the simple steps outlined under "How to Know Your Purpose." Don't be in a rush, but start the process of discovery today. What's holding you back?

EIGHT

RUNNING ON EMPTY

Don't get to the end of your life and have God tell you that you lived the length of your life, but you didn't live the width or the depth.

—*Kami Pentecost*

It was as hot as Hades, and I literally could see the heat waves bouncing off the boulevard. Thankfully, my baby-blue 1976 Plymouth Duster had air-conditioning, and it was blowing at full blast, but I was still sweating like a racehorse. Dressed in long pants, a long-sleeved shirt, and a tie, I was on my way to work. This was not my usual summer attire and *not* what you'd want to wear on a day with triple-digit heat, but it's what you do when your boss says, "Dress professionally, or don't show up to work." (For the record, and in my humble opinion, whoever created the necktie is a sadist. Seriously, what purpose do they serve besides causing misery?)

Then it happened. My engine started to spit and sputter, and the car lurched as if someone were trying to grab the back bumper and stop me. In a panic, I looked at the gauges and was shocked to see the gas level read EMPTY. You've got to be Chevying me! Not good. Not today. Not now. I barely made it to the side of the road where I had to leave my car and hoof it the last mile to work.

It doesn't matter how new or cool your car is. When you're out of gas, you're out of luck. Running on empty sucks.

ANOTHER LESSON LEARNED THE HARD WAY

In January of 2003, I became the founding pastor of Eastpoint Church in Spokane Valley, Washington. After a couple of years of getting the new church up and running, we outgrew our leased facility and needed a new church home. It was an exciting challenge, and I threw myself into the search and then into the renovation of a Kmart. (Yes, we are the original Blue Light Special church.) For the better part of six months, I went without a day off, and on a regular basis, I engaged in hours of hard physical labor assisting as much as I could with our remodel. It was exhausting but fun.

The move into our fresh church digs brought new folks to the church, and we hired new staff to accommodate our growth. Things were humming, and life was good. However, friends and family kept asking me, "Are you okay?" At first, I just blew them off, but after about the tenth time, I started to get irritated. *Why is everybody picking on me? Why can't they see all the great things God is doing and leave me alone?*

Frankly, I look back now and realize I was running on empty. It doesn't matter how cool your church is, or how big your staff is. When you're out of gas, you're in trouble. I finally started to figure this out when our first youth pastor resigned and left poorly, and I wanted to hurt him. It became even more apparent to me when Sunday became the worst day of the week for me (not okay when you're a pastor). I didn't want to get out of bed. I didn't want to pray. I didn't want to preach. I didn't want to do anything but be left alone. I came to a point of despair as a pastor. Yep, running on empty is bad—very bad.

In the next chapter, I'm going to share about creating margin and embracing Sabbath rest, both of which I miserably failed to do in this season of my life. But here's what I hope and pray you'll understand now: For you to consistently live an uncommon life of hope, you need God's power. You can't do it on your own. In your strength, ability, and power, you can go only so far and do only so much.

CRACKED POTS

As strong as you might think you are, on your best day, your power matched up to God's strength is like a triple-A battery compared to a nuclear reactor. Your energy is limited and easily drained; God's is not. Life drains you. Struggle and hardship bleed you dry. Living in a busted and imperfect world with broken and flawed minds and bodies taps your spiritual, emotional, and physical resources. Life's battles can result in hopelessness.

The life of the apostle and the first missionary, Saul of Tarsus (later known as Paul), has always inspired me. No one would argue that Paul lived anything but an uncommon and extraordinary life. He is a superb model to all of faith, hope, and obedience. However, Paul understood the source of his power. He wrote these words: "But we have this treasure in jars of clay to show that this all-surpassing power is from God and not from us. We are hard pressed on every side, but not crushed; perplexed, but not in despair; persecuted, but not abandoned; struck down, but not destroyed."[65]

Simply put, Paul said this treasure—our relationship with God and His glory and presence in our lives—is found in common, ordinary, and even weak bodies. The reason? So that a watching world will know that it's God's power at work, not ours. How did Paul survive pressure, perplexities, and even persecution? Not by his might, but by the favor of God—"this all-surpassing power is from God and not from us." He understood that because we are common pots of clay

65 2 Corinthians 4:7–9 (NIV).

(and most of us are cracked pots), we desperately need a frequent refueling of God's Spirit.

Too many Christians live with a power loss rather than an ongoing power encounter with the Holy Spirit. We're running on empty and trying to git-r-done on our own. And this is tragic because we need the Holy Spirit's empowerment to *be* the people God has intended us to be and to *do* the work God has intended for us to do. This is why Paul also wrote, "Be filled with the Spirit."[66] In fact, he implies that we must *continually* get filled up with the Spirit and power of God. In other words, we need regular and consistent refueling.

FATHER, SON, AND THE OTHER ONE

My friend and author, Dr. Jeff Kennedy, wrote a superb book about the Holy Spirit.[67] In Jeff's book, he says, "The contrast between powerless American religion and the first-century church is startling." Sad, but true. New Testament believers had absolutely no expectation of doing anything great for God without the touch of God. Why do we think we can operate in our strength and our abilities without God's help? Why do we independent and stubborn American Christians think we can do the work of the kingdom without the power of the King? The Holy Spirit is not just "the other one." He is the very presence and manifestation of God in us to guide and empower us. Without His abiding power, a consistent epic life of uncommon hope is impossible.[68]

Jesus told His disciples to stay in Jerusalem until they were "clothed with power from on high," and He also told them they would "receive power when the Holy Spirit comes."[69] Wisely, they waited together until they received the promise. Why don't we?

A young man in his twenties named Ben came to me some time

---

66 Ephesians 5:18 (NIV).

67 Jeff Kennedy, *Father, Son, and the Other One* (Lake Mary, Florida: Passio, 2014).

68 John 15:5.

69 Luke 24:49 (NIV); Acts 1:8 (NIV).

ago frustrated with his lack of spiritual progress and deeply disappointed in his religious journey. He told me, "I pray a lot, I read the Bible every day, I fast, and I memorize scripture, but my life in Christ seems empty and without much joy."

First, I asked him if he had any unconfessed sin in his life. He assured me that he was far from perfect, but he wasn't rebelliously holding onto anything. I believed him. He was sincere and seemed genuine in his desire to walk with Jesus.

Next, I asked, "Ben, has anyone ever told you about the role of the Holy Spirit or about what it means to be full of the Spirit?"

He gave me an uncomfortable look and said, "Uh, no, but I'm not into that 'wildly costal' stuff." (In his opinion, most Pentecostals were wild holy-rollers swinging from the chandeliers.)

"I'm not into weird and whacky either," I said. "But, Ben, God's power is provided in and through the work of the Holy Spirit in our lives. Yes, we need the community of faith, and we need the Word of God. And yes, we certainly need to fast, pray, and practice all the spiritual disciplines. But unless we are Spirit-empowered, we will not and cannot fully live the life Jesus has planned for us. God knows how weak we are, and how incapable you and I are of accomplishing all that He has planned for us without a regular infusion of His power."

TIME FOR A CHANGE

So many people are trying so hard, and they're so exhausted because they've not tapped into the source of God's strength. You and I urgently need the Holy Spirit so we can worship. We need Him so we can do the work of God. We need Him if we are to walk in hope regardless of our struggles. It is the influence of the Holy Spirit that transforms us from the inside out. And without question, to do the supernatural, we need the Holy Spirit who is the giver of God's good and perfect gifts.

So, how can we know and experience more? Here is the first thing to consider: You'll *want* more power when you see that you *need* more power.

Why do triathletes train? Because they know they need to if they are going to finish the race. Why do pregnant women typically eat healthier? Because they know there is a precious life growing within them who needs proper nourishment. Why do northwesterners, like me, drink a lot of coffee? Because we need to in a climate where it's dark at 4 PM in the winter! (There's a reason why Starbucks started in Seattle.)

Most of you don't need a lot of motivation to do the things you recognize as necessary for life. No one has to twist your arm to eat, sleep, or play. You typically find a way to do what you want to do, especially when it's a matter of life or death. Being filled with God's Holy Spirit is of similar importance. For us to do the impossible, to go beyond our natural and limited abilities, we require God's divine empowerment. When you see that reality, you will be hungry for more of the Spirit.

Again, the apostle Paul knew his desperate need, so he wrote, "I came to you in weakness with great fear and trembling. My message and my preaching were not with wise and persuasive words, but with a demonstration of the Spirit's power, so that your faith might not rest on human wisdom, but on God's power."[70]

Paul said, "I know how feeble I am without God's help." Do you? If not, may I humbly suggest that perhaps you don't feel the need for more of God in your life because you're not taking any great risks for God? Stop and think for a moment: When was the last time you did something at least a little bit risky for God? Have you recently stepped into the often-uncomfortable realm of walking in faith? In the pursuit of an epic life filled with uncommon hope, you'll have to step into the unknown and uncomfortable at times.

---

70 1 Corinthians 2:3–5 (NIV).

ASK FOR MORE

Here's something else you should know about the Holy Spirit: You'll have more of Him and get more power when you ask.

Can't a sovereign God do whatever He wants to do and give us whatever we need whenever we need it? Yes, but throughout the Scriptures, we see God's desire for our cooperation and partnership with Him.

- Abraham became the father of faith because he chose to believe and obey.

- Noah and his family were spared destruction because he labored to build the ark.

- Esther saved her people because she broke the rules and entrusted her life to God.

- Jeremiah became a prophet because he said *yes* to God's call.

- The disciples of the New Testament (including Paul) spread the good news because they cooperated with and functioned in the power of the Holy Spirit.

Just before His crucifixion, Jesus taught His disciples about this collaborative work, and He described it as abiding or remaining in the vine.

> Get your life from Me, and I will live in you. No branch can give fruit by itself. It has to get life from the vine. You are able to give fruit *only when you have life from Me*. I am the Vine and you are the branches. Get your life from Me. Then I will live in you and you will give much fruit. *You can do nothing without Me* (John 15:4–5, NLV, emphasis added).

The word picture Jesus uses is that of a branch receiving its life from the vine. In fact, without staying plugged in, the branch produces no fruit and eventually withers and dies. God wants to work with us, in us, and through us. He doesn't want to make us do anything; He does, however, want us to choose to dwell in Him and therefore to flow in His life and power.

By the way, Jesus has promised that when we ask the Holy Spirit to fill and empower us, we can be confident that God hears and answers that prayer.

> So I say to you: Ask and it will be given to you; seek and you will find; knock and the door will be opened to you. For everyone who asks receives; the one who seeks finds; and to the one who knocks, the door will be opened.

> Which of you fathers, if your son asks for a fish, will give him a snake instead? Or if he asks for an egg, will give him a scorpion? If you then, though you are evil, know how to give good gifts to your children, how much more will your Father in heaven give the Holy Spirit *to those who ask Him*! (Luke 11:9–13, NIV, emphasis added).

When the cry of your heart is, "Oh, God, I need more of your Holy Spirit and more of His power in my life," God smiles and answers your plea.

A LOW RUMBLE OF THUNDER

Many years ago, I attended a conference in Denver, Colorado. It was another time in my life during which I was empty and withering off the Vine. At the end of the service, the speaker invited people forward for prayer. He said, "If you're feeling empty and dry and you want more of God's power in your life, come." I felt like this guy was reading my mail; he described me to a T, so I went and I waited on God.

To explain what happened next is difficult. At first, it was like a low rumble of thunder in the distance. I knew God was working in my heart, but it wasn't that overwhelming or powerful. Then, the speaker prayed, "God, these men and women have come to you, not to me! And they have come thirsty for Living Water and hungry for more of you. Come, Holy Spirit." Within moments, I began to weep, which then grew into sobs, and I ended up on my face wailing. The low rumble in my heart became a mighty rushing wind of the Spirit.

I chose to come forward. I responded to a call to cooperate with God. Then God met me with His power like lightning bolts to my soul.

As I was on my face crying and shaking, a young teenage girl knelt down beside me and prayed, "Give him more, Holy Spirit." That's all she prayed, but she must have asked God to do so a dozen times, and each time she did, another bolt struck. It was indescribable, and I left that place with a Rocky Mountain Jesus high.

Are you hungry? Do you want more? Are you desperate for power? Simply ask—right now—for the Holy Spirit to fill you to overflowing. You may not end up on the floor blubbering, but God will hear and answer you, and that's not my promise—it's His.

A KINK IN THE HOSE

There's one more thing I want to cover before we move on, and it's essential. Yes, you need to *want* more and *ask* for more, but sin can hinder the flow of God's power in your life. Don't misunderstand me; it's not that we can ever earn God's favor, blessing, or power. We never deserve it, and His goodness in our lives is always a gift of His grace. But we can quench, reduce, or hinder what He wants to do through us if we rebelliously hold onto sin.

Unconfessed sin or any sin from which we have not repented is like a kink in a hose that can stop the flow of God's life and power through us. Again, quoting Dr. Jeff Kennedy, "Your greatest barrier to the fullness of life in the Spirit is fear and sin." In other words, the problem is never on His end; it's always on ours.

The fact that we can hinder the Spirit's work in and through us is precisely why the apostle Paul warns, "Do not quench the Spirit."[71] And right in the middle of Paul giving extremely practical instruction regarding how we are to live as Christ followers, he also wrote to the church in Ephesus, "Do not grieve the Holy Spirit of God."[72] God's power is readily available to each of us, but we can mess that up with stubborn and unyielding hearts.

Many years ago, I had one of the most amazing overseas ministry trips of my life. I had the privilege of serving with a dedicated group of Christians and leading worship in several gatherings in Scotland and England. Our team director, Clint, was an incredibly gifted leader and speaker. Watching him inspire people to pursue God's kingdom and seeing God's power demonstrated through his prayers was mind-blowing. Several times, I thought, *Father, make me like Jesus and Clint!*

Several months after we returned home, the sad news broke that he had some serious character flaws and moral issues in his life. I was devastated and confused.

"Excuse me, God, how in the blazes did Clint function with the kind of power and anointing I saw in him when he had that much sin in his life?"

The Lord spoke to my heart. "Imagine what I could have done and would still be doing if it weren't for the hidden sin in Clint's life." Wow. That's a lesson I hope never to forget. God wants to do phenomenal things through our lives if only we will own our crap and confess it rather than denying it and hiding it.

God wants us to know more of His supernatural power. He wants us to operate in His fullness rather than run on empty. At the center of living an epic life filled with joy and hope is our desperate need for

---

71 1 Thessalonians 5:19 (NIV).

72 Ephesians 4:30 (NIV).

more of Him and His empowering touch. In our limited strengths and abilities, we can go only so far.

To be all that God wants you to be, and to do all that God wants you to do, you must remove the kinks that hinder Him from flowing freely through your life. To live the uncommon and extraordinary life He has planned for you requires an awareness of your need, a willingness to walk in the Spirit, and the guts to admit your sin humbly.

My prayer for you echoes Paul's prayer for the church: "Be strong in the Lord and in His mighty power."[73] You can't change what's going on around you until you start changing what's going on within you. And here's some incredible news: You can change. Really. In Jesus, the impossible becomes the Himpossible.

---

73 Ephesians 6:10 (NIV).

EPIC STEPS

- Do you feel like you're living with a power loss or a Holy Spirit-powered infusion in your life? What's your action plan to help you avoid running on empty?

- Do you feel plugged into the Vine (Jesus) or unplugged? Why? Is there a kink (i.e., blockage) in your soul? What can you do to release the flow of God's Spirit in your life? Ask God to reveal any area of your life where you need more of His power.

NINE

TURTLES ARE NOT MUTANT NINJAS

It takes a lot of slow to grow.

—Eve Merriam

Sometimes we think experiencing the abundant life in Christ means living hard and going fast. In our Western culture, speed is typically synonymous with impressive. Unfortunately, buzzing through life often gets us nowhere—or lost. As Rollo May once said, "It is an ironic habit of human beings to run faster when they have lost their way."

Ask anyone who knows me, and they will tell you I talk too fast and move too quickly. Frankly, sometimesmymouthspeaksfasterthanmybrainthinks (and apparently, I type that way at times too). In my world, quick is good and supersonic is better. I hate to be late, so I rush just about everywhere. I've been that way for a long time.

My first car as a sixteen-year-old midwestern boy was a 1967 Pontiac Bonneville. My dad and I found it nearly destroyed in a used car lot in Duluth, Minnesota. However, after a lot of time and way too much money, it became a beautiful cherry-red, two-door convertible, four-speed manual 389 sports coupé with glass packs. It was loud and fast. I could lay a patch of rubber while shifting into third gear and reach sixty miles per hour in about ten seconds. You don't even want to know how many times I got pulled over in that dream car.

For years, I owned a Vulcan Classic 1500 motorcycle, and there's nothing quite like speed on a bike. I've had that baby up to almost 120 miles per hour, and I was smiling the whole time.

Fast and furious. That makes me happy. However, a truly epic and hope-filled life is rarely lived in the fast lane. (You might want to slow down and read that last line again.)

Some of you move through life thinking it's a race. You're burning rubber and power-shifting hard trying to get to the next adrenaline rush. You don't have time for anyone who can't keep up with you. Anything that gets in your way gets demolished—quickly. You press the limits, thinking to yourself, *I'll do whatever it takes to have whatever I want, and nobody can stop me!* The problem is you're running on fumes, and you think that's a good thing.

MUTANT HEROES?

As boys, my sons used to watch a Saturday morning cartoon called *Teenage Mutant Ninja Turtles* (TMNT). The stars were four teenage turtles named after Renaissance artists—Leonardo, Michelangelo, Donatello, and Raphael. Of course, being a responsible father, it was necessary for me to watch this show with my sons occasionally. I had to protect my kids from any potential heresy and make sure they weren't exposed to unnecessary violence. (I might be smiling right now.)

My youngest, Isaac, was enthralled with TMNT. In fact, after almost every program, he would go ninja on his siblings as he yelled, "Cowabunga, dudes! Let's kick some shell!" It was hilarious and annoying. In my great wisdom as a young sensei father, I once tried to explain to him, "Isaac, turtles are not really violent, they don't move like lightning, and they don't eat pizza."

His reply was classic. "Dad, they're mutants. Of course they do!"

How do you reason with a starstruck boy?

Sadly, in our culture, we tend to make heroes out of mutants. We think the multimillionaire executive who works eighty hours a week is a superhero. The famous coach or player who lives on the road more than they live at home is someone too many wish they could become. We admire the politician or pastor who sacrifices all for the sake of the masses. We envy the Grammy-winning performer even though he or she lives without any margin and in dread of the paparazzi.

In our saner moments, we ask, "How do they do it and survive?" But with our next breath, we whisper, "I wish I was famous."

How do you reason with a starstruck adult?

We think jet-setting will make us happy. But a good life is rarely lived at Mach one or without any room to breathe.

THE OTHER "S" WORD

I was first introduced to the concept of living with margin when I read Dr. Richard A. Swenson's book, *Margin*, back in the late nineties. A friend gave it to me as a birthday gift. I love to read and devour books, but I wasn't happy when I read the subtitle: *Restoring Emotional, Physical, Financial, and Time Reserves to Overloaded Lives.* I thought my buddy was suggesting I was a workaholic. And to add insult to perceived injury, he said, "You need this book! I think it will change your life."

For some reason, I wanted to go ninja on him and yell, "Cowabunga, dude! I'm going to kick your shell!" However, he was right, and I needed to carve out some space in my life. Swenson, in fact, defines margin as "the space that once existed between us and our limits."[74] In other words, without at least a little distance between what we *can* do and what we *should* do, we are on the brink of a disastrous overload. We all need a little wiggle room, and that open space

74 Richard A. Swenson, MD, *Margin: Restoring Emotional, Physical, Financial, and Time Reserves to Overloaded Lives* (Colorado: Navpress, 2004).

in our lives doesn't hinder us—it enhances us. In fact, if there weren't margins on the pages of this book, you probably wouldn't have made it this far reading it. Even our eyes need space in which to rest.

Let's hit the way-back button and take a look at something God implemented thousands of years ago. It's called the Sabbath. Hang in there with me; I promise this won't hurt (well, maybe a little).

God set His people free from bondage to the Egyptians. Some time later, He gave them some basic yet important rules to adhere to in the Ten Commandments. The fourth commandment says, "Remember the Sabbath day by keeping it holy."[75] God went on to explain that He had provided the children of Israel six days in which to do all their work, but the seventh day was His and a day of rest. The word used here in the Old Testament is *shabath*, and it means "to intercept or interrupt." It clearly implies a complete cessation of normal and regular activity. For the Jews, Sabbath was the practice of setting aside one day a week to take time out from life's busy duties and demands. Sabbath is the one occasion in which your work is done, even if it isn't.

The concept is ancient, and for many, the practice is forgotten or ignored. It's a simple thing to understand but a difficult thing to do. However, God commanded His people to hit the pause button and produce nothing one day each week. It's the one time when taking a break is more important than work. It's an entire day that is to be holy (i.e., set apart) for the Lord.

If by nature you're lazy, this might be good news because it means there are fifty-two days a year when you can be a toadstool and not feel guilty. But if you're a workaholic and you tend to go full throttle twenty-four-seven, then you're probably speed-reading this section and rationalizing your craziness.

---

75 Exodus 20:8 (NIV).

THE PROBLEM WITH CRAZY

When you live a crazy life, you lose perspective. You often find it impossible to know peace. Everything and everybody are flying past the window of your heart so fast it all becomes a meaningless blur. Without margin, there tends to be little joy or hope in your life. Delight is found in the quiet places of your soul, and it is best experienced in times of reflection and rest. Margin leads to moments of hope, because sometimes it's the only place where you can breathe.

As previously mentioned, I used to backpack on a regular basis. Glacier National Park is, without question, one of the most beautiful places on earth. Nestled in the northern Rockies of Montana and Alberta, Canada, it contains over one million acres of spectacular terrain. It's hard to describe a place so amazing that it leaves you speechless.

We hiked all day, and I was exhausted. It's tough carrying a sixty-pound pack on a winding trail with elevation. Furthermore, most of that day, it rained hard, but the more significant problem was I started that trip dead-dog tired. I had been living fairly consistently on the edge of burnout.

Just as the storm stopped, we reached our destination; it was a campsite at the base of a place called Hole-in-the-Wall. The site is located in a meadow carved into Mount Custer. This incredible area is reached only on foot, and it includes waterfalls, alpine gardens, and a host of wildlife, from grizzlies to mountain goats.

We set up our tents, and since it was only late afternoon, my companions decided to do a little exploring and rock scrambling. I was too pooped and decided to stay back at the camp.

It was so quiet and so peaceful. Extraordinary beauty surrounded me. The only sound I heard was a gentle breeze blowing through the alpines. I sat on a log rubbing my tired feet when an old hymn came to my heart, and the melody burst from my mouth:

All Creatures of our God and King
Lift up your voice and with us sing
Alleluia! Alleluia!
Thou burning sun with golden beam
Thou silver moon with softer gleam
O praise Him!
O praise Him!
Alleluia! Alleluia! Alleluia![76]

What happened next blew my mind. As I sang that ancient song, three mountain marmots came out of their burrows and just sat there and watched me. For a moment, I felt like I was in Narnia and they might join me in four-part harmony. It was awe-inspiring.

When the show was over, they nodded in appreciation and scurried off, but my soul was full. For months, I'd been pushing hard and exhaling every ounce of gusto and energy in me. Now, however, and for the first time in a long time, I was inhaling life, and it was restorative.

Hurry hurts. Rest restores. In fact, one of my favorite authors, John Ortberg, once put it this way: "Hurry is not just a disordered life. Hurry is a disordered heart."[77] That day at the base of Hole-in-the-Wall, a hole in my heart was repaired. That kind of healing happens only in the margins of life, in those quiet places where you decompress.

SOMETIMES LESS IS MORE

God wants you spiritually, relationally, physically, and emotionally whole. That's always been His desire. Where did we get the foolish idea that it's better or more spiritual to go, go, go until we're empty?

---

76 *All Creatures of Our God and King,* words by Francis of Assisi, circa 1225.

77 John Ortberg, *The Life You've Always Wanted: Spiritual Disciplines for Ordinary People* (Grand Rapids, MI: HarperCollins, 2006).

I love what Anne Lamott once wrote: "Almost everything will work again if you unplug it for a few minutes, including you."[78]

Yep.

The hard part is unplugging in an over-plugged culture.

On any given day, we are often overwhelmed with all the noise and activity of life on planet Earth. We live with the radio or TV continually blaring while our smartphone keeps alerting us to a million text messages. Tragically, we keep trying to cram as much as we can into every moment of every day, but our over-productivity becomes counterproductive. More is not always more; sometimes less is more.

My friend Wayne Cordeiro once said, "The road to success and a nervous breakdown is often the very same road." Like lemmings (small rodents that have been known to follow each other as they charge to their deaths off the edge of cliffs), we too often mindlessly follow the over-amped behaviors of the masses as we fall to our emotional death in the process. But that is so *not* what God wants for you and me.

The "abundant life" of hope that Jesus wants for us is epic, but not insane.[79] It is full, but not crammed. In fact, Jesus said, "Come to me, all you who are weary and burdened, and I will give you rest."[80] Sabbath. Margin. Rest. This is the pathway to a truly holy and healthy existence.

HOW DO I GET THERE FROM HERE?

Maybe you've noticed that *knowing* and *doing* are sometimes two very different things. I can know that bacon is bad for me (some of you just panicked), but if I love the pleasure of copious amounts of pig fat more than I love low cholesterol, then doing something about it is highly unlikely.

---

78 Anne Lamott, *Almost Everything: Notes on Hope* (New York: Riverhead Books, 2018).

79 John 10:10 (NIV).

80 Matthew 11:28 (NIV).

Most of us know we need downtime. We know that running on empty is a recipe for disaster. Even if we're not very religious, we understand the idea of Sabbath. The problem comes in carving out the time for recovery and refreshment. And let me be clear: It never happens by accident and only becomes a reality when we get intentional about creating margin in our lives.

For years, I thought about running a marathon. I'd been a casual jogger for a long time and always thought it would be cool to run 26.2 miles. (You might be thinking, *Now I know this guy is whacked! Who runs that far for fun?*) Yes, it is extreme, but I wanted to do it. However, doing so requires a lot of preparation. Nobody wakes up one day and says, "Hey, I think I'll go for a four-hour run."

Without a doubt, we live in a microwave world. We want everything now and with as little effort as possible thank-you-very-much! But there's nothing quick or easy about preparing to run 138,000 feet (give or take a foot or two). I read half a dozen books on running marathons. I watched training videos about preparing for long-distance running. I talked to people who'd run marathons. I created a training timetable. But even all of that wasn't enough. At some point, I had to put on my running shoes and get my butt out on the road. Strategy and knowledge are worthless without action. As it turns out, I've finished two marathons, but that would never have occurred without hitting the pavement on a regular basis.

In a similar way, creating margin in your life starts with a plan, and it only happens when you decide to work your plan. What will you do today to create space in your life? What has to happen for you to find a Sabbath this week? (For the record, your Sabbath doesn't have to be a Sunday; mine isn't.)

If you look at my calendar, you will find both daily and weekly time allotted for rest. Every Friday, for the sake of my ongoing mental and spiritual health, I go unplugged. I turn off my smartphone, tablet, and computer. The only way to get in touch with me on my day off is to show up at my door, and you better have an excellent reason for being there if you do.

Every day, I also carve out micro-Sabbath moments. A micro-Sabbath is anywhere from five minutes to an hour in my schedule. My calendar simply says "appointment," and the appointment is with myself. Sometimes those minutes are invested in prayer. Often, I use them to read. Occasionally, that time is spent taking a power nap. There's nothing like a quick nap to rejuvenate your mind and body.

My Friday Sabbath and these daily micro-Sabbath experiences provide me with a way to intentionally slow down and to practice the unhurried life that promotes hope. They are an important means for me to refuel my tank and reset my heart. By the way, this is *not* selfish or lazy—it's godly and wise.

Some of you have denied yourself a break because you think it's unspiritual when, in fact, you are never more spiritual than when you are full and rested. An empty person is a weak person destined for breakdown and failure, and an easy mark for the enemy.

One last thing: I know that you might own a business or work in a high-demand field (like a doctor or a CPA during tax season), and you're thinking, *This just isn't possible for me!* In case you're wondering, being a pastor could easily be a twenty-four-seven occupation. I understand your struggle. But if you want to survive and thrive, if you want to truly live an epic life of purpose and hope, and if you want to live beyond your fifties—carve out a Sabbath. Don't wait for it to magically occur. Make it happen. Grab your calendar and block out time for you to rest. Have the long view, and I promise you the world will keep moving while you're not.

ACE, THE HELPFUL PLACE

I am the polar opposite of a fix-it guy. Frankly, I'm a break-it moron who has almost no mechanical ability or manual dexterity. Following directions has never been my forte, especially when someone who speaks English as a second or third language writes them.

Without hesitation, I will pay somebody to repair whatever I've broken or to put together the new grill from Ace Hardware. For a guy like me, Ace is awesome. Unlike some hardware and home-supply stores, Ace is known for providing helpful advice to novices like me. I will pay twice as much to buy it there than I might at the local Home Depot. I don't care. Just don't ask me to use a screwdriver or wrench (though I am exceptionally gifted with a hammer; I just beat things into submission).

I have a toilet that's been running for a long time. Yes, I know, it's a waste of water. Yes, I know, it's easy to repair a running toilet (unless you're me). Yes, I know, I should call a plumber. Instead, the last time I was at Ace, I bought a new set of guts for my bowl. For months, however, the package has sat there on a table in my garage mocking me. One of these days, I'm going to give it a shot, but I dread it because I know how frustrating it will be. I may come close to losing my salvation. The problem? Fixing stuff drains me (no pun intended), and the only day I typically have enough free time to tackle it is on my one day off. *Sigh*.

What drains you?

What person, task, activity, or experience tends to suck the bone marrow right from you?

What empties your tank?

I know we'll still have to deal with the reality of doing difficult things we dread at times, but you can't be in leak mode all the time and thrive. Remember, recuperation happens when you cease from life's regular duties and struggles. In the place of those things, do whatever builds you up.

So, what fills you up? What helps you feel alive and refreshes your soul? Don't wait for a convenient time to engage in these life-giving activities.

Do them now.

Do them often.

Here is a profound paradox: *Life is too short to live it too fast.* So don't just stop once in a while to smell the roses; instead, take the time to plant a rose bush and invest in your future.

Please don't let life kill you. God never meant for you to live as a mutant. And for the record, most mutants are hopeless creatures.

Let's take a look next at another challenging issue that robs us of our hope: waiting.

EPIC STEPS

- Do you take a regular Sabbath? Is it truly a day when you "produce nothing" and rest? If not, what needs to happen to make this day of rest happen in your life?

- Do you believe that "sometimes less is more"? If not, why? Make a list of the things that consume a lot of your time. Do you see anything on this list that you can stop doing and still be fine?

- Make a list of the things that drain you. Make a list of things that refresh and refuel you. If there's a lot more on the first list than the second, what needs to be done to change this in your life?

TEN

WAITING IS NOT FOR WIMPS!

It's easy to trust God when he does what we want;
it's the other times we grow.

—*Bob Goff*

Most of us hate the word *wait*. It's a four-letter word that stirs up all sorts of negative emotions. No kid likes to hear, "Wait your turn." No adult likes to wait in long lines at the DMV. No husband enjoys waiting for his wife to do "just one more thing before we go." No wife loves waiting for her husband to fix the toilet that's been running for months. And I've never met anyone who appreciates it when they feel God is saying, "Not yet. Wait."

In our minds, waiting ranks right up there with a root canal. Necessary, perhaps, but not at all fun. And waiting is often a hope-killer.

If you've had to wait for a doctor (and we all have), imagine waiting for word from your doc about cancer. As I mentioned in chapter six, I am a cancer survivor. If you've had cancer, or know someone who has, you understand that a considerable part of this battle with the "C" word is the agony of waiting.

After a disturbing conversation with my family doctor about the possibility of cancer, I had to wait to see the specialist. Then I waited to hear what he thought about my blood test results. The urologist wanted to do a prostate biopsy, so I waited for weeks to get that procedure. Then I had to wait to find out the results. In fact, the three days between that very invasive and painful biopsy and finally hearing from the doctor were the longest days of my life.

When the diagnosis was cancer, I waited for the surgery. After the surgery, I waited to find out how things went and to know the prognosis for my future. And then, for over six years, I had to wait for annual blood test results to see whether I was still cancer-free or not.

Okay, I'll own it: I despise waiting. Going slow is difficult for me, but waiting is painful. And what's more, I'm often terribly impatient. Whether I'm waiting in a doctor's office, waiting in line at the store, waiting for my IRS refund, or even waiting at a red light, waiting irritates me. A lot.

WAITING ON GOD

The most difficult challenge for me, and maybe for you too, is waiting for God. We pray. We fast. We search the Scriptures for a promise. We vow to God to be better and to do better, believing that somehow we can twist His arm into action. We desperately look for something, anything, to hang our hope on. We cry out to Papa God for answers, and we curse the heavens when He seems silent.

A dear friend of mine has suffered from infertility for years. She's tried everything, read every book she could get her hands on, talked to multiple doctors, and attempted several expensive medical procedures. She and her husband have the medical bills to prove it. And yet nothing has changed. No pregnancy. No baby. No answers. And hope is waning.

A man I met recently has spent the better part of the last four years writing a memoir. He's a good writer. He's done his research and paid his dues as a newspaper journalist. The manuscript is a well-written tale mostly based on his experiences at a small Christian college. It's an intriguing and inspiring story of rediscovering his faith amid a backdrop of what some would call spiritual abuse. However, week after week, he gets rejection letter after rejection letter from publishers who say, "Good writing, but there's no market for your book." His dream of publishing is fading.

A thirtysomething woman I know is single and frustrated. She's intelligent and gifted; she's attractive and full of life. She's tried online dating sites and a few blind dates that were set up by friends. She's even met a couple of guys her mom thought were perfect for her, yet they weren't. (Seriously, Mom?) At this point, all she wants is to be a wife and a mom, but both of those dreams seem elusive. She sometimes cries herself to sleep at night wondering what's wrong with her and why she can't find the man of her dreams. She's lost hope.

There's a little boy who is very special to me. He was born with a serious heart condition that requires him to undergo regular testing. If his heart doesn't improve as he grows, he'll need surgery to survive. His amazing parents have done everything they can, including praying constantly. Yet every year, they wait for another doctor visit, another test, and another report that, one way or another, will affect their son for life.

Waiting is hard. It hurts. We want to believe God has a plan. We pray for patience and perspective. But the passing of time is painful.

At the heart of this issue is more than just a struggle with patience. We find it hard to wait because sometimes we find it difficult to trust God.

We lie awake in the darkness wondering . . .

Has God forgotten me?

Have I brought this pain upon myself because I'm a failure?

Do I not deserve what I'm longing for, or am I being punished?

Does God have my best interest in mind?

Can He be counted on to make good on His promises?

Does God have any idea what I'm going through?

Is God even listening to me?

I'VE GOT THIS!

Sometimes, our confusion, fear, and lack of trust immobilizes us. We feel like a confused squirrel on the road, not sure if we should stop, go back, or press on, only to find ourselves ending up as roadkill.

Often, we humans are inclined to take matters into our own hands. "God helps those who help themselves," we've been told, and that leads us to take action. Is it a premature, impatient, and foolish action? Probably. But we are tired of sitting on our duffs waiting for God to act, so we do.

Maybe you've heard of a guy named Abram (later renamed Abraham). His story is found in the book of Genesis. He was, without a doubt, a man who loved God. Long after his death, he would be known to many as the "father of faith." However, Abe wrestled with waiting, and sometimes he failed pathetically, just like you and I do.

In Genesis 15, Sarai (later called Sarah) was barren, and Abram complained to God about not having a son. At that time, the only heir he had was a servant. Here's the promise he received:

> Then the word of the LORD came to him: "This man will not be your heir, but a son who is your own flesh and blood will be your heir." He took him outside and said, "Look up at the sky and count the stars—if indeed you can count them." Then He said to him, "So shall your offspring be."[81]

No doubt about it, that's an incredible promise. God guaranteed Abram not just a son, but offspring as numerous as the stars. I imagine a smile the size of the moon on the face of old Abe.

What's more amazing is the fact that Abram took God at His word. Verse six says, "Abram believed the LORD, and He credited it to him as righteousness."

Well, he had hoped, believed, and trusted God.

Until he didn't.

---

81 Genesis 15:4–5 (NIV).

About ten years went by, and Abe wasn't getting any younger, and his wife was still barren. I struggle to wait ten days, so I can't imagine how difficult it was to wait ten years. Then Sarai came up with a plan to help out God and her husband.

"Hey, Abe! Check out my maidservant, Hagar. She's young, ripe, and ready. How about you and I have a surrogate child through her?"

"Uh . . . Let me get this straight, Sarai: You want me to have a second wife and have sex and a baby with her? Is this a trick question?"

Here's the story from Genesis 16:1–5 (NIV):

> Sarai said to Abram, Now Sarai, Abram's wife, had borne him no children. But she had an Egyptian slave named Hagar; so she said to Abram, "The LORD has kept me from having children. Go, sleep with my slave; perhaps I can build a family through her."

> Abram agreed to what Sarai said. So after Abram had been living in Canaan ten years, Sarai his wife took her Egyptian slave Hagar and gave her to her husband to be his wife. He slept with Hagar, and she conceived.

> When she knew she was pregnant, she began to despise her mistress. Then Sarai said to Abram, "You are responsible for the wrong I am suffering. I put my slave in your arms, and now that she knows she is pregnant, she despises me. May the LORD judge between you and me."

For ten years, they had waited. For ten long years, Abram and Sarai had dreamed of having a son. For ten excruciating years, month after disappointing month, Sarai had wept a little louder and longer each time her cycle came. Until enough was enough, and they decided to do what to them seemed like a good idea at the time.

They had hope, faith, and trust.

Until they didn't.

And for the record, this part of the story didn't end well. Hagar and her son, Ishmael, eventually were exiled, and Ishmael's descendants were at odds with Abe's other offspring for millennia. (Check out Genesis 21.)

I wish I could shake my head in disgust at Abe's impatience. However, I've been there and so have you. Too often, we decide to step in and help God out, and we end up with our own Ishmael story.

ROOFTOP MELTDOWN

In my first book, I shared openly about my time as a prodigal. I'd gone to Bible school and had been a staff youth pastor at a large church. But for a season, I walked away from God because I became angry and bitter. Naturally, I also left the ministry, and I ended up working in the banking industry in a variety of jobs over about a ten-year period.

Just about everything I put my hand to in banking succeeded. I advanced quickly and made good money, but I was miserable. I worked hard, and my bosses loved me, but God created me to be a pastor. Don't misunderstand me: There's nothing wrong with being a banker—unless you're running from God as Jonah did. And I was sprinting.

After my return to faith, I thought I'd return to full-time pastoral ministry soon. In fact, I so desperately wanted to be a pastor again that I started a new church as a bi-vocational pastor. I worked forty-five to fifty hours a week in banking and an additional fifteen to twenty hours a week trying to build a church.

I failed. Miserably.

I wouldn't quite call the church I began an "Ishmael," but it wasn't a "promised son" either. After a couple of years, we merged our little band of misfits with another slightly bigger church filled with more broken people. In many ways, that merger was a blessing, but it was still painful for me and I was so disappointed.

About that time, Laura and I decided to move our entire family of six over three thousand miles from Southern California to Southern

Florida to help with a relatively new church in Boca Raton. Our parents thought we were crazy. We probably were.

The church was growing and thriving, and life was exciting, but I continued to work in banking, and I still hated it. Our only car was an old Cadillac with a broken air conditioner (not a good thing in Florida). I managed the item-processing center for the bank and worked the swing shift. Every day in my forty-five-minute drive from Boca to West Palm Beach, I'd complain to God.

God, this drive in ninety-degree weather with 100 percent humidity is killing me.

Uh . . . God . . . you know this ain't what I want to do for the rest of my life, right?

Come on, God, how long are you going to make me do this when all I want to do is serve you?

The only thing I loved about my job was the daily helicopter pickup of checks from the roof of our building. The bag of checks was flown from West Palm to a central processing center in Miami. Every day, toward the end of my shift, a helicopter would hover over the pole with the bag attached to the top. Somebody had to take the bag to the roof and run it up the pole, and because I love helicopters, typically I'd do the duty. This meant waiting for the scheduled pickup and hanging out on the roof for ten minutes or so.

In the evening, except for mosquitoes the size of flamingos, Southern Florida is heaven on earth. Enjoying an ocean breeze, I'd stand on that rooftop and soak in the stunning view. However, instead of being thankful for my little piece of paradise, I'd moan and grumble some more to God.

One evening as I waited on the roof, I began to cry. My Christian boss had ripped me a new one in a not-so-Christian way earlier that day. Two of my female employees hated each other, and both of them resented me. One of them had called in sick for about the tenth time that month, and I knew it was the "green flu." (This ailment is similar to the "blue flu" police officers sometimes have when they call in sick in protest, but "green flu" is reserved for bankers.)

I was mentally exhausted and spiritually spent. My crying turned into weeping, and that turned into sobbing. For a split second, the thought of jumping off that roof crossed my mind. I felt hopeless.

I wailed, "How long, Lord? How much more of this do I have to endure? How much longer do I have to wait to be fully restored to pastoral ministry? I'm tired of trying to keep everybody else happy when I am so miserable!"

My meltdown wasn't pretty.

And during that display of self-pity, God spoke to my heart.

How long will you reject what I am attempting to do in your life through this season of waiting? Stop striving to please others and start pleasing me and only me.

Ouch. I didn't need any clarification. I knew at that moment that God was much more concerned with my character than He was with my comfort. It was time to embrace the wait rather than to resist it and miss what God wanted to do in my heart and character.

It's difficult to describe what happened next, but I ended up on my knees surrendering.

I surrendered my expectations.

I surrendered my demands.

I surrendered my timeline.

I surrendered my heart and character to the chiseling work of God's Spirit on my soul.

And surrender is the path to hope and peace.

Almost another year passed before I ended up on staff at a church in full-time ministry. It wasn't an easy year. I still had moments during which I'd try to crawl off the altar of surrender. However, my heart and mind had been changed on that rooftop, and I knew in my know-er that it was a defining experience in my journey. I'm also certain it would have taken a lot longer to be restored as a pastor if I had rejected God's Word to me that day in West Palm Beach.

Your issue might be something completely different than mine. Maybe your struggle has nothing to do with your vocation or calling. Maybe it's about a longing for marriage or children. Maybe it's about a battle you've fought for years with your health. Maybe you believe God gave you a promise that is so elusive it now fills you with resentment rather than the hope it once brought into your life.

Regardless of the circumstances, we all face the same question: Will you trust God to create His masterpiece in and through you, or will you demand to be the master of your fate? Will you trust Him and put your hope in Him, or take matters into your own hands? Will you believe Him and wait for the promised son, or will you create an Ishmael?

WHAT IT TAKES TO WAIT

Here are some practical things I've learned along the way about waiting. Are these things easy? No. Are they worth it? Absolutely.

First, you have to determine *now* what you will do during a postponement of your dream. Don't wait to the point of frustration to decide how you will handle the delay, or you're going to be in trouble. It's best to understand early in the process that God's sense of timing is radically different from ours. Unlike you and me, God sees the end from the beginning. Unlike us, God is just as concerned about what happens along the way, as He is the result. In fact, sometimes the journey is more important than the destination. Go figure.

During the delay, my faith and character were forged. By choosing to trust in Him after that experience in West Palm Beach, I learned firsthand that God doesn't help those who help themselves. God helps those who rest in and rely on Him. I didn't always understand, the waiting was still agonizing at times, and there were many other moments of struggle. However, my perspective had changed. I had begun to see waiting in the same way one might see the cooking of stew—the longer the wait, the better the flavor.

Second, to wait for Him means to engage in your present circumstances with joy. Rather than miss what's happening right now because you're so preoccupied with your future, God wants you to be fully present in the moment. Sadly, while waiting for God to do the one thing or the big thing I desperately desired, too often I missed a thousand little things that mattered to Him.

I can only imagine how different many of my years in banking might have been if I had consistently embraced them as an opportunity to intentionally represent the Father at any given moment. I regret that I didn't typically see my coworkers or the many employees I had over the years as people God put in my life for a unique purpose.

Instead of resisting and resenting the process of waiting, choose to look for God every day and to find His purpose in the present.

And finally, for you to wait with patience and hope, it's always best to have someone in your corner encouraging you to hold on. Unlike Sarai, who injected her ideas into Abram's struggle, my wife, Laura, consistently inspires me to keep my eyes fixed on Jesus. By her example and her words, she frequently reminds me that God is good, He is faithful, and He always has a plan. She challenges me not to let the known and the seen world discount what God is doing in the unseen realm. My amazing wife is a woman of great faith who always points me to a place of hope.

Frankly, you will wait more successfully when you find a partner (e.g., a spouse, best friend, or even a close family member) who will stand with you in the darkness and confusion and whisper into your soul, "It's okay. We're not alone. God is here and near."

I find strange comfort in Abram's humanity. This man, who later became the father of faith and an epic hero to countless millions, struggled and failed just like we do.

It seems that victory and failure often go together in our spiritual journey. Sometimes we wait for God, and we grow. Sometimes we act impulsively and rashly, and we still grow, but it just takes longer. And sometimes, we fail miserably, but even then, God is patient and good and able to redeem any situation and any broken life that is surrendered to Him.

There's that word again: *surrender*. For a Christ follower, surrender and trust are interwoven. You can't succeed at one without the other. And trust me, relinquishing control and yielding to God is the best path to an epic life of uncommon hope.

EPIC STEPS

- What have you been waiting for from God? Make a list of the things you're struggling to believe will ever come to pass.

- Honestly consider: Have you given up? Have you taken matters into your hands (and out of God's)? Have you grown bitter or better in the waiting? What must you do to have a change of heart?

- What hope or dream do you need to surrender again to God and His timing?

ELEVEN

HOPE IN THE FACE OF THE UNEXPECTED

If you lead well, you will lead change. If you lead change, you will be criticized. If you can't take criticism, don't lead.

—*Thom Rainer*

One of my oldest friends and a longstanding member of our church called me. "Hey, Kurt, can we grab lunch together soon?"

"Sure," I said, but knowing what was coming sent me into a tailspin of depression rather than anticipation. I'd heard from others he was upset and was leaving our church.

Later that week, over a bowl of teriyaki chicken and rice, he assured me his exit had nothing to do with me. He talked on and on about needing some time and space to "discover his path" and to find out what he believed about the church. But what he was telling me didn't line up with what he was telling others. He told his friends he was disappointed with my leadership.

I didn't see that coming.

Not too long ago, I got a call from another friend. "I'm done! I'm getting a divorce! Cory has cheated on me." We wept together on the phone, and I knew their marriage was over and there was nothing I could do.

I didn't see that coming.

A few months back, a Facebook friend request popped up on my computer. It was from an old high school buddy. He also sent me a message. "Bub, you're never going to believe who's walking with Jesus now: ME!" Of course, I accepted the request and messaged back, "That's so awesome! You were the last guy I'd ever expected to become a follower of Jesus!"

Nope, I didn't see that coming, either.

I'm not sure why the unexpected continues to surprise me, but it does. After sixty-plus years of life, you'd think I'd have this figured out: I should expect the unexpected.

On a regular basis (like, weekly) something happens to me that surprises me. Sometimes it's a pleasant surprise, and sometimes it's not, but I can't tell you how many times I'm faced with something and think, *I didn't see that coming!* And the unexpected events often try to rip hope from my heart.

GOD'S UNEXPECTED ADDITIONS

Steve and Mary were an incredible couple and active in our church. They had two adorable daughters and life was good. Then one day, God began to tug on Mary's heart about officially pursuing adoption.

Even before they got married, they had talked about adoption because Steve's dad and Mary's sister were adopted. When I spoke with them about their journey, Mary said, "We were comfortable with two kids, and we both had some serious concerns over the cost. At first, we were talking about international adoption, which is very expensive."

They knew the risks. They understood the financial and personal costs. But neither one of them could ignore what God was doing in their hearts.

About that time, there was a series at Eastpoint about saying *yes* to God. They told me, "God used that series of talks to challenge and encourage us to press through our fears and worries." One day, after many hours of discussion into the wee hours of the night, Steve said to Mary, "Hey, let's look into foster-to-adopt."

And so began their unexpected adventure.

Everyone told Mary it would take at least three months to complete the foster licensing process, but for them, the entire approval process only took forty-five days. In fact, the period between their decision to open their home and the moment of their first placement was relatively short.

In the spring of 2009, James entered their lives. His placement was supposed to be only for five days, but before long, the state asked them if they would be willing to be a permanent option. Another unexpected moment in Steve and Mary's life.

James's adoption was finalized when he was fifteen months old. He became a beautiful part of their forever family, and they were thrilled and satisfied with three children.

However, when James was twenty-two months old, they got a call while on a Disneyland vacation. "Would you consider another permanent placement?" James had a newborn brother, and the state went to Steve and Mary first because the baby was a sibling.

As Steve put it, "We went home with a different Disneyland 'souvenir' than we expected—another addition to our family." Their second son, and James's biological brother, Jeff, became a part of their growing family.

UNEXPECTED HARDSHIPS AND BLESSINGS

Sometimes, when God asks us to do something, we step into the unknown and the unexpected in faith but with some unrealistic expectations of Him. I'm afraid we too often anticipate God's "blessings" will bring us a lot of warm fuzzies and a life of ease. We reason, *God is good, and He's asked me to do something good, so certainly my obedience will always feel good and make me happy.*

Not necessarily.

Steve and Mary have no regrets. Given the opportunity to do it all over, they both said they'd do it again without hesitation.

But it hasn't always been easy.

- Their parents are supportive now, but they initially had strong reservations and concerns.

- At first, their closest friends had mixed feelings and did not know how much emotional support to provide.

- Social get-togethers became more difficult with the boys' special needs.

- Mary loved her job as a fitness instructor at the local gym, but she gave that up to focus on her four children.

- The boys' physical and emotional challenges meant the family wasn't always able to make it to church.

- They had to learn how to keep their marriage healthy and how to carve out "adult time," which wasn't always easy to do.

- Perhaps the biggest challenge Steve and Mary faced was learning how to parent and advocate for children who'd experienced trauma and who were not typical kids.

When I spoke with them about their adoption journey, they said, "Unless you've done it, you just don't get it. And that's a hard reality to face with family and friends."

Nonetheless, Steve and Mary would be the first to tell you of the many joys they've known. Their oldest daughter Ann, has become an excellent caretaker, especially for babies with special feeding needs, while their other daughter, Michelle, now has terrific compassion for people in need. (They attribute this to their family adoption experience.) They smiled with tears in their eyes as they said this: "We have two little boys we immensely love, and God has used us to change the trajectory of their lives."

God has also used this couple as a catalyst to get other people to foster and adopt. Mary and Steve have learned skills they teach and give away to others, even professional teachers. In fact, they now help coordinate an annual conference about adoption and foster care that has inspired and helped hundreds of families.

Steve recently told me, "I've stopped trying to figure out how much is enough or how many kids we will have. We don't have a 'plan' anymore except to be available and to keep saying *yes* to God."

I happen to know their latest foster child started out as a three-day respite care baby, but they've had him for ten months now, and he may very well end up in this extraordinary family as another forever child.

Steve and Mary's story is a remarkable example of how God seemingly delights in stretching us to do the difficult and the impossible as we embrace the unexpected.

OUT OF OUR COMFORT ZONE

Perhaps you're starting to see a pattern. We plan our perfect little lives. We organize, schedule, calendar, and structure our world to align with our expectations. Life might not be perfect, but we're generally satisfied and happy. Then, God does something or says something completely outside of our little box.

In fact, the Bible is full of examples of God surprising people.

- "Hey, Abe, I want you to leave your home and go to a strange and foreign land."

- "Yep, Gideon, I've chosen you, the least of the least, to lead my army into victory."

- "Ruthie, I know Boaz might not have been on your short list for potential husbands, but he's the guy I want you to marry."

- "Sure, David, you're the youngest and the runt among your brothers, but I want you to be king over my people."

- "Yeah, I know, Jerry, you're just a teenager, and you don't like to speak in public, but you're going to be a prophet to my people."

I could go on and on. I haven't even gotten to the New Testament yet and the long list of men and women who were utterly shocked by Jesus's call.

A WEE LITTLE MAN

Throughout most of my years growing up in elementary school, I was short. Short-tempered, shortsighted, and short in stature. I was still growing when I got married at eighteen. (For real.)

I used to hate it when my friends would ask, "How come you're so short?" Like I had some deep and profound philosophical answer to their stupid and rather hurtful question.

I didn't.

"I don't know. Guess I'm just special" was my standard reply.

They didn't buy it.

Neither did I.

This part of my past may, however, explain my early fascination and connection to another height-challenged guy by the name of Zacchaeus. His story is found in Luke 19.

Unfortunately, besides being a wee little man, he was also a tax collector. Not a good job in Jesus's day or ours (my apologies to any IRS employees), but at least Zach was successful. And rich. Though he was considered a cheat and a traitor.

Being short and despised is tough.

But one day, Rabbi Jesus came walking through Jericho, Zach's town. Undoubtedly, he had heard the rumors about this great teacher and miracle worker.

Zach was also curious. *Who is this guy? How did some blue-collar carpenter from Nazareth get to be so popular?*

Doctor Luke writes that Zacchaeus wanted to "see who Jesus was, but because he was short, he couldn't see over the crowd."[82]

I hate it when that happens.

So did he.

Perhaps Zach thought, *We short people may not be tall in size, but that's never stopped our giant ability to see the big picture. I know what I'll do! I'll get above these punks and grab a bird's-eye view.*

So, he ran his stubby little legs as fast as he could and climbed up into a sycamore fig tree to see Jesus.

"Brilliant and doable," he reasoned.

We have no concrete information about Zacchaeus other than what the Scriptures tell us. But I imagine ole Zach to be a middle-aged, pot-bellied, well-dressed guy with a bald head. I chuckle when I see this image of an old, short guy running down the street, with his robe drawn up in his hands, and in a hurry to get to his spot in a tall tree.

Then, in my mind's eye, I see him struggling to grab a low-hanging branch, drenched in sweat and breathing hard.

But the best is about to happen.

Jesus stops right under him, looks up, smiles, and says, "Zach, come on down! Let's hang out together over some matzo ball soup and babka!"

Zach didn't see that coming.

Neither did the crowd who moaned and muttered, "Jesus has gone to be the guest of a sinner."

It turns out, from that moment on, everything changed for Zacchaeus. This unexpected encounter, from an unexpected perch in

---

82 Luke 19:3 (NIV).

a tree, and then a completely unexpected invitation from the Rabbi, turned this cheat into a champion for God.

And, quite frankly, Jesus's last statement to Zacchaeus still surprises a lot of religious people. "The Son of Man came to seek and to save the lost."[83]

Nobody saw that coming.

FOUR WAYS TO RESPOND TO THE UNEXPECTED

By now, I hope you see it's better and wiser to expect the unexpected. However, it's also important to understand how to respond (rather than react) when life throws you a shocker.

Here are four things that will help you:

First, *stay tender*. Difficulty has a way of leading us into cold-heartedness. When we get smacked in the head or the heart with something we didn't see coming, we can become mean and emotionally ugly. Wouldn't it be great if struggles and trials always brought out the best in us? In reality, the opposite tends to happen: we go sour and act foul. Don't go there; stay tenderhearted.

Second, *stay faithful*. I suppose being faithful can mean a lot of things to people. Here's how I see faithfulness defined in the Bible: To stay faithful is to stay true, trustworthy, reliable, and committed. So, when the unexpected comes, one of the great tests you will face is this issue of faithfulness. Will you remain loyal and stay the course—no matter what? When surprised, you can react in fear or respond in faith. For the record, faith is always best.

Third, *stay aware*. Never forget you are in a spiritual battle. Sometimes the unexpected happens because we live in a broken world filled with broken people. Sometimes it happens because we make boneheaded decisions. Sometimes, however, what is unexpected to

---

83 Luke 19:10 (NIV).

you is a diabolical plan of the evil one, Satan, who hates God and wants to control you.

Peter warns us, "Be alert and of sober mind. Your enemy, the devil, prowls around like a roaring lion looking for someone to devour. Resist him, standing firm in the faith."[84] It's bad enough hard things happen, but when we fail to recognize the source of evil, we end up fighting the wrong battle. When we forget we're in a spiritual battle, we too often use human weapons against others rather than spiritual weapons, such as prayer, against our real enemy. By the way, resistance is not futile if we are fighting the enemy with all we have in Christ.

Finally, *stay teachable, and you will grow*. One of life's greatest truths is you and I grow best in a crisis. I don't like that reality. I wish it weren't that way, but it is. Once again, unexpected situations and difficulties can make us bitter or better. We can *go* through the struggles or *grow* through the struggles.

In fact, the only way to "count it all joy," as James suggests, is to have a radical change in your perspective regarding trials.[85] The unexpected can be a tool that shapes and builds you rather than a hammer that demolishes you. It's up to you to choose.

HOW WILL JESUS SURPRISE YOU?

I have no idea what's going on in your life right now. I don't know if you're in the best or the worst days of your life. I don't know if you're lovin' life or have lost hope and are thinking about ending it all. I have no way of knowing what's ahead for me, let alone you.

Sometimes, I cry out to God in a mix of anger and despair. "I don't know how much more of this I can take. Why is life so crazy? Why are people so difficult? Why didn't I see *that* coming? Why am I so stupid sometimes?" (Yes, I get somewhat raw with God at times.)

As I write this, I'm at the end of a long week filled with a boatload

84 1 Peter 5:8–9 (NIV).

85 James 1:2–8 (ESV).

of unexpected struggles. What's more, I was wondering about the weeks to come. Then God quietly spoke to my soul.

When have I ever abandoned you?

Where have I ever led you astray?

Name a moment in your past when I screwed up.

I Am That I Am, child.

I am here.

I am not finished with you yet.

I am worthy of your trust, so lean into me and rest.

Kurt, I've got this.

I've got you.

And He does.

I'm still learning that I am not *I Am*, and I have to expect the unexpected. To do any less is unwise, because life is full of things you and I will never see coming. If my hope or yours is based on the success of our neat and tidy little plans, then we're set up for failure. But if we choose to fix our eyes on the God of hope, our circumstances might not change, but we sure will.

So, once again, the choice we face is to become either bitter or better. We can drift into despair or get drawn into God's presence and find hope. We can resentfully fight the unforeseen, the unexpected, and the inevitable, or embrace the fact we are not all-knowing. And that's okay because He is.

Maybe, like Zacchaeus, you feel as if your circumstances are bigger than you, and you're struggling to see the point. Perhaps, like my friends Steve and Mary, you keep running into the unexpected.

Please remember:

Jesus is trustworthy.

He's faithful.

He's got this.

He's got you.

And becoming a person of uncommon hope means accepting your humanness and your limitations as you surrender each day to the One who loves you more than His own life.

EPIC STEPS

- Make a list of a few things in your life that you didn't see coming (i.e., unexpected moments). Put a star by the events that surprised you even though today all is well. Put a check by the experiences that didn't end up becoming a blessing (at least so far).

- Now, honestly reflect on this: Regardless of the outcome on this side of eternity, are you more like Jesus because of what's happened in your life? Are you bitter or better? And what perhaps needs to change in your heart regarding your past disappointments?

- Review the "four ways to respond to the unexpected" and consider how to better stay *tender, faithful, aware,* and *teachable* in your current or future struggles.

TWELVE

MY LEFT FOOT HAS BEEN TO TIBET

You didn't come this far to only come this far.
—Jennifer Dukes Lee

Fernanda was a petite little village girl with a smile you could probably see from space. She wore a white dress (I think it was white) that looked like it hadn't been washed in weeks, but it was her smile and her big brown eyes you noticed first and foremost. She was adorable.

I first saw her when she stuck her head through an open window where I was volunteering as a dental assistant in the jungles of Guatemala. The second time I saw her, she was playing with some other kids on a swing set that looked older than dirt. Fernanda also had an infectious giggle.

This poor, grimy little girl of five or six stole my heart. By our standards, she had almost nothing, but in some ways, she was far richer than you or I. Her joy and hope were not based on material possessions. Rain or shine (both of which are abundant in Guatemala), she lived each day with joy. Regardless of her limited educational and vocational opportunities, she lived without worry or hopelessness.

For the previous week or so, I'd been with a medical mission team serving in small villages. I worked as a volunteer assistant with the dental team, which meant I spent a lot of my time cleaning dental tools—ew! On my feet all day in 90-degree heat and 90 percent humidity meant I sweated buckets. It was both grueling and glorious.

The villagers are incredible people. Most of them live in huts with wood slats for siding and palm tree branches for a roof. They cook over a fire, and tomorrow's dinner is usually running around the yard (and I use the word *yard* loosely). Most of them don't have a car, so they walk. A lot. Everywhere.

I have a deep love and respect for Guatemalans. They are a strong people who have learned to survive amid hardships that would kill most North Americans.

To say I was entirely out of my element and comfort zone would also be true. I'm a pastor. I don't have any medical training. I speak just enough Spanish to get into trouble and to find out where the bathroom is located. Honestly, I like the heat, humidity, and the rain, but not being able to communicate is frustrating. After all, I speak and write for a living.

I was in my late fifties at that time, with a bad back, messed-up knees, and the smallest bladder in the world, and making a mission trip was difficult. But it's good to step out of my safe world and go to places that require sacrifice. (There's that word again.) It would be easy, too easy, to send others and to remain in my little church bubble, but that's not where I grow. True for me; true for you.

One of the lessons I learned again on that trip was how much God loves the poor. It's true that poverty can crush hope, but God promises those in need will not be forgotten.[86] His compassion for them is unquenchable.

I've also noticed how often God shows up in His power to heal those who have relatively nothing. I've prayed for hundreds of people over the years, and most of the legit miracles I've witnessed happen for

---

86 Psalm 9:18.

people who are desperate because they don't have access to modern medicine the way you and I do.

A couple of ladies on our team and I spent one afternoon going to several huts. Part of our task was to give people water filters and to show the villagers how to set up and use them. After explaining everything, we always asked, "How can we pray for you?" They don't hesitate to tell us about various illnesses, and these desperate people welcome our prayers with hearts filled with hope and gratitude.

The first home we stopped at held a woman who was in her early forties, and she had eight children. When I asked if she had any needs for which I could pray with her, she rattled off several. She had pain in her head and severe pain in her back. She also asked us to pray for her husband who wasn't a believer. She said, "My husband is a drunk, and I want him to know my Jesus so he can be set free."

I laid one hand on her head and the other on her back, and through an interpreter, I prayed. It's hard to describe, but I could feel the healing presence of Jesus. She started to cry, and after I prayed, she gave me an enormous smile and a hug.

The next day, she came by our makeshift clinic, and we found out two things had happened. First, her pain was gone. All of it. Completely. And at almost the same time we were praying for her the day before, her husband was praying with another team member back at our temporary medical center to become a Christ follower!

God loves the poor.

God loves the desperate.

God loves to show up on the backside of nowhere and bless people who have nothing.

Before I move on, let me be clear here: You don't have to go to the jungles of Guatemala for God to use you. However, if you want to walk in hope, you must discover your God-given purpose, and that purpose probably includes loving the poor or doing something else that might surprise you.

MO MUST GO

Do you remember Moses and the burning bush?[87] God showed up when and where Moses least expected, and it changed the course of history for the Israelites. Moses was on the backside of nowhere. He'd gone from being the prince of Egypt to shepherding goats. (Nothing against goats or shepherds, but Moses wasn't exactly living the high life of royalty.) For forty years, he'd probably wondered, *How did I end up here?* I'm sure there were many times when Mo felt low. Hopelessness must have been a frequent reality for this guy who'd once had it all.

Nelson Mandela once said, "There is no passion to be found in settling for a life that is less than the one you are capable of living." Without question, Moses lived without passion for a long time because he was capable of far more than herding animals.

Again, I'm not sure why, but as I mentioned in the last chapter, God loves to surprise us, and our destiny is sometimes discovered when and where we least expect it. After Moses finally stopped arguing with God—and accepted his call to set the Israelites free from their bondage—I can only imagine the hope and sense of purpose that started to grow in his heart.

Maybe God's not done with me yet?

Maybe I can still make a difference?

Maybe my life will finally count for something?

My point is simple. You don't need a burning bush to give you hope, but you may need an encounter with God. I know that sounds a bit mystical. I also understand a fiery bush encounter (or whatever it is for you) isn't something we experience every day. I do, however, believe God is so kind and so faithful and so good to us that He will do whatever it takes to get our attention. He's committed to you. He wants you to have the hope of a dream that is bigger than you.

Jesus might call you to serve the poor. He might challenge you to fight human trafficking (a modern-day way to set people free). God

---

87 See Exodus 3.

might give you a burden for the illiterate or the disabled. And His invitation may come through an unexpected encounter.

When it comes, argue less and go more, because hope is often found in the going.

GOD, THIS IS CRAZY!

I met a Nepali man named Batsa many years ago. He lived in Kathmandu, was a Christian, and directed a Christian orphanage. He was speaking at a pastors' gathering in Portland, Oregon, and sharing about his ministry in a country extremely hostile toward Christians. His plea for prayer and support moved me, but I didn't do much. They took an offering for him, and I think I threw ten dollars in the offering bag.

About a month later, I was praying about some of the financial struggles we were experiencing at our small church in Portland. I wasn't thinking about Batsa. I wasn't thinking about his ministry; I was thinking of mine. More specifically, I was complaining to God about the lack of money in our church bank account.

At that moment, and to my utter surprise, God showed up and I saw a picture in my heart of Batsa and what I assumed to be many children in Nepal. I started to weep. Honestly, before that time, I'd never really thought much about the poor. But the images in my mind wrecked me (in a good way).

Through my tears, I said, "What do you want me to do, God? I don't have a lot of money. We're a small church, and I'm a nobody from nowhere." (A bit like Moses, I was arguing.)

My wife, four kids, a variety of rodents, and I all lived in a run-down, hundred-year-old farmhouse. I drove a twenty-year-old Dodge. There were times when the church had to delay my meager salary a week or more. From my perspective, our lack of resources clearly let me off the hook regarding any kind of financial support for Batsa.

But at that very moment, the Lord spoke to my heart: "Empty

your bank account and ask your friends and family to support you. I want you to take the money to Batsa in Nepal personally."

"Uh, God, that's crazy. Nepal is on the other side of the world. If Christians are not liked, pastors will be hated. And I'm sure Batsa would rather have the money I'd spend on an airline ticket than me showing up." (I continued my excuses.)

I couldn't shake it. I couldn't deny it. For reasons far beyond my comprehension, God wanted me to go. And three months later, I sat next to my brother Kraig as we landed in Nepal.

My time with Batsa and the orphans in that mysterious and marvelous city of Kathmandu changed me. It was there among some of the poorest of the poor that God gave me His heart for them. He gave me a passion for serving and caring for them, and God gave me a massive deposit of uncommon hope. That experience was nearly twenty-five years ago, but I was forever transformed. I began to have faith that God could use me—a poor, simple nobody from nowhere—to make a difference.

A FRIENDSHIP BRIDGE THAT WASN'T SO FRIENDLY

A year or so after my first trip to Nepal, I took a second, and this time with a small team from my church. We felt led to go to the rural communities outside of Kathmandu where conditions were truly awful. The capital city has many destitute people, but the small villages of Nepal are occupied by the poorest of the poor. Most live in brick-and-stone homes sometimes smaller than my three-car garage. The floors are often dirt. There's no central heat, they cook over fires, and nobody has running water or electricity. Every village child I saw had a runny nose. Every adult looked twenty years older than they were, and though they always smiled, their eyes looked tired and sad.

We had a driver take us to the border of Tibet and Nepal high in the Himalayan mountains. There is a bridge on that worn-out road in a trekker's village called Kodari that is a link between Nepal and Tibet (technically, China now). This bridge over the Sun Kosi River is a ragging torrent of extremely cold water from snowmelt. The whole scenic experience is breathtaking. Imagine being at just over eight thousand feet high, the air is thin and always brisk, yet the smell of cooking fires is everywhere while you are surrounded by the Himalayas that soar above the clouds. This setting on our planet may not be one of the seven natural wonders of the world, but it's incredible. How could this spot of so much natural beauty be a place of such horrible human struggle?

One more piece of trivia: Tibet is under Chinese rule, so Americans aren't allowed to cross the bridge—oddly enough called the *Friendship Bridge*—unless they have a visa.

I know.

I tried.

But I was stopped by a small and stern-looking Chinese military man, who stood in my way. He just shook his head no and pointed back to the Nepal side of the bridge. In a moment of stupid defiance—I don't know why I do things like this—I slid my left foot over the borderline. For about a second, I was in Tibet! At least until the army dude stepped closer and raised his gun. I immediately smiled, bowed, and turned around quickly as I walked back to my friends, who shook their heads in irritation at me. There was no need to start an international incident with the Chinese when I was there to help the poor.

The plan was to walk back from the border to the city. It was a distance of about one hundred miles on a road more trail than street. We walked about twenty miles a day, always at high elevation, and it was exhausting.

Nonetheless, we walked, and in every village along the way, we stopped and I preached the gospel through an interpreter who traveled with us. We also offered to pray for the sick, and we saw people healed. People cried at the kindness of the silly Americans trekking through their village, loving on them and praying for the sick. It was powerful and amazing to see God work in the lives of these poor people, many of whom had never heard the name of Jesus.

LESSONS LEARNED IN THE HIMALAYAS

I can't tell you of any lasting spiritual fruit in the lives of the villagers of Nepal. As far as I know, only one man prayed with us to become a Christ follower.

But I can tell you what God did in me.

I am now willing to go anywhere, to anyone, and to do anything God asks.

I haven't complained about my lack of resources for a long time. Coming face-to-face with severe poverty permanently alters your perspective.

I also learned obedience to God doesn't always make sense to our human way of thinking, but it is a path I have never regretted taking, even when it's a path near ten thousand feet high in a strange land.

And, most importantly, I have found that uncommon hope and an epic life come to those who go wherever God sends them regardless of the personal cost.

Something profound happens in us when we have an encounter with God that redirects the trajectory of our lives—when we step out in faith to obey and follow Him.

God will get your attention any way He can.

He wants to use you to make a difference.

He's committed to you discovering and engaging in a dream that will probably blow your mind.

What will you do when your "burning bush" happens?

EPIC STEPS

- Has God ever asked you to do something that didn't seem to make any sense on a human level? Did you obey the Lord? If so, how did that experience affect you and change the trajectory of your life? If you didn't obey, have you confessed your sin to Jesus? It's never too late to grow.

- Heart check: Are you holding onto anything (or anyone) that might keep you from a life of surrender the next time God speaks to you? And do you have God's heart for the poor? If not, ask Him to give you His compassion, and see where that might lead.

THIRTEEN

ONE TRULY IS THE LONELIEST NUMBER

In a futile attempt to erase our past, we deprive the community of our healing gift. If we conceal our wounds out of fear and shame, our inner darkness can neither be illuminated nor become light for others.

—*Brennan Manning*

The majority of you reading this are divorced. That's a statistical reality in our country. If you are not divorced, you are the child, sibling, parent, or close friend of someone who's gone through this trauma.

The sad reality of the pain caused by divorce isn't something we can ignore, shrug off, or deny. It hurts. Divorce devastates relationships, profoundly wounds people, and often leaves individuals hopeless—at least for a season. This is why the Bible says, "God hates divorce."[88] To be clear, He doesn't hate divorced *people*, but He hates what it does to the people He loves.

From time to time, I'll see a couple on a television show or a

---

88 Malachi 2:16 (NKJV).

movie act as if going through a divorce is no big deal. Frequently, divorced couples are portrayed as kind and even loving to each other. The people seem fine with what's happened and almost cavalier about the whole experience. However, nothing is further from the truth in the real world.

IT SUCKS!

My parents were divorced. I have siblings and a daughter who are divorced. And I've pastored hundreds of couples through this dark valley. Without question, and regardless of the cause or even if there's a biblical reason for the breakup, divorce always leaves people wounded and bleeding. Always.

Yes, there is hope after divorce (and I'll get to that in a bit), but nothing shreds our hope and joy faster or worse than the destruction of our most intimate and sacred human relationship.

Sally was a beautiful woman. She married James after a relatively long engagement. They both had promising careers, lots of money, and a bright future. I did their premarital training. I officiated at their wedding. If you'd asked me, I would have told you they were destined for a long and happy life together.

However, about eight years into their marriage, everything started to unravel. James traveled too much for work, and he was rarely home with Sally, so she was lonely. They both allowed their communication to grow stale and shallow. Sunday was generally the only day James was home, and he was always exhausted. Too tired to go to church. Too spent to have a meaningful conversation with his wife. The only thing they did together every Sunday was sex, but even that was boring and unfulfilling for both of them. James said he wasn't ready to have children. Sally was no longer sure she wanted any kids with him as the father. James was gone too often and was too emotionally detached.

In every way, they lived a married-single lifestyle. Same home.

Same bed. Same bank account. But their emotional, physical, and spiritual connectedness was barely existent anymore.

One day, at Starbucks, a man in line smiled at Sally (I'll call him Buddy). It was the sort of smile James used to give her when she walked into a room. She smiled back, and he offered to buy her a cup of coffee. Innocent enough, at first, but then she started showing up at the same time every day looking for Buddy, and she was disappointed when he wasn't there.

This casual and relatively safe coffee relationship went on for weeks. Then, after many flirtatious encounters, Buddy suggested they get together for lunch. They did, and lunches became dinners, and dinners eventually became sleepovers. Sally felt that everything she didn't have with James she had now with Buddy.

When James and Sally ended up in my office regarding their marriage issues, it was too little too late. He was mad and hurt. She was cold and done. Within six months, they got divorced, and it was ugly. Accusations were made—some true and some false—but the words stung like an angry hornet. Both of them were emotional wrecks.

They had to sell their incredible home for far less than the market merited. They lost most of their mutual friends who were too uncomfortable with how things ended. And perhaps saddest of all, Sally married Buddy, but that marriage lasted less than two years. What starts poorly often ends poorly.

What began as a relationship of oneness for Sally, first with James and then with Buddy, ended in a thousand broken pieces.

ONE IS NOT SAMENESS

When two become one, that doesn't mean they lose their identity or uniqueness as an individual.[89] Marriage is not a shapeless blob that consumes a person's distinctiveness. Blobs are ugly; marriage is beautiful. So, oneness does not mean sameness. I am remarkably different

---

89 Matthew 19:5.

from my wife, Laura. However, at a deep level, we were united and became one in marriage. Physically, emotionally, and spiritually, we were and are connected and bound. We have exclusive access to each other with our bodies through sex, and we have intimately opened our hearts to each other by being naked of soul. No one knows me better or more intimately than my wife.

- Laura often knows what's on my mind before I do.

- She sees all of my faults and knows most of my failures, but she loves me, nevertheless.

- After forty-plus years of marriage, our bodies are quite different than they were when we got married, but we choose to love the wrinkles now too. (After gaining some weight, I often remind her there's just more of me to love now than there used to be.)

- My wife understands my dreams and empathizes with my frustrations and disappointments.

- She knows I hate tomatoes, and I know she loves them! (For the record, in my mind, a tomato was the actual forbidden fruit of the garden.) But what's even better is she doesn't ever give me grief for being a vegetable-hating beef-eater, and Laura just smiles when I remind her veggies are for rabbits.

We are still one because we have worked at it over the years. In fact, our oneness is better now than ever.

REALITIES OF THE HEART

We humans often tell ourselves, and others, it's too late, that our marriage or our situation is impossible. However, if God is in the mix, a miracle can happen. And because of His involvement in your life, there is always hope for your marriage.

I have seen some remarkable things happen when we invite God into our mess. I've seen marriages that were dead be revived (like mine several decades ago). I've seen people overwhelmed with hardship find hope.

Ty and Karen are a great example of God's power to heal. From the beginning, their marriage was rocky. In fact, while they were engaged, both of them slept with others. From their perspective, though they never talked about it, they believed until they were married and had officially "tied the knot," they were free to fool around. They saw sex as a recreational activity. Somehow, in their minds, unlimited sex in marriage would curb their wandering hearts.

When they came to talk to me at the suggestion of a mutual friend, Ty admitted to having sex with multiple partners multiple times in the three years they'd been married. Karen said, "I've only been unfaithful twice, but I've flirted with just about every guy in my office."

I said, "So, how's that working for you two? Did sex outside of your marriage help it or hurt it?"

With their heads hung low, they both muttered, "We're a mess, and probably beyond repair."

I had the privilege of leading them to a relationship with Jesus, and I told them what I'm telling you: God can heal your marriage. It's never too late or beyond repair when God is part of the equation. And Jesus did restore Ty and Karen's marriage.

Whatever we take to God and surrender to Him becomes an opportunity for the miraculous. As Jeremiah put it, nothing is too hard for the Lord.[90] However—and this is important to understand—God will *not* override a hard heart. He will not force you or anyone else to do the right thing. Which means, quite frankly, although God is able to help us, we can distance ourselves from His power by our pride and blinding stubbornness.

---

90 See Jeremiah 32:17.

There's a verse in Revelation that is fairly well-known and often taken completely out of context. Jesus is speaking to a church and Christians when He says, "Here I am! I stand at the door and knock. If anyone hears my voice and opens the door, I will come in and eat with that person, and they with me."[91] The big idea here is that when we fail (and we do), we are to repent and change our hearts. However, Jesus isn't going to knock down our door and bolt into our lives like SWAT on a raid. We can be stubborn and hard-hearted, or we can humble ourselves and let Jesus in.

For heaven's sake, Jesus wants to have prime rib and garlic mashed potatoes with us, but we must choose to let Him into our lives.

James and Sally are a sad example of a married couple who didn't try to get help from a pastor or counselor until they hated each other. Again, it was too little, too late. Not because God was limited, but because they were. Their hearts were hardened.

Ty and Karen are proof that God can and will do the miraculous in any marriage surrendered to Him.

I repeat: Nothing is too hard for God. However, a hard heart leads us down a path that rarely ends well. And that's not God's fault; it's ours.

THE SOLUTION SIDE

So, what can you do to avoid finding yourself in a bad situation where your marriage is hurting?

Here are some helpful insights from the book of James.

First, change your perspective regarding your trials.[92] As I wrote in chapter one, life is hard. Relationships are difficult. Sure, sometimes things are relatively easy, for a while, but a struggle is just around the corner. Recognizing this reality will encourage you *not* to be proud

---

91 Revelation 3:20 (NIV).

92 James 1:2–4.

and stubborn when life hits the fan. It's okay; trials happen. Stop being embarrassed by your brokenness, failures, or messed-up life.

Next, humble yourself early in the struggle, and get support.[93] We are all pushing a rock uphill at times, so it's okay to get help, and it's better to do so early. Too often, I hear couples say, "We can't afford a marriage counselor!" I remind them a counselor is far cheaper than a divorce.

Another vital part of the healing process is to keep short accounts and develop good conflict resolution skills. The book of James challenges us to be quick to listen and slow to speak.[94] When you're hurt, disappointed, or mad, don't react—respond. And don't wait too long to have a healthy conversation with the offending spouse. The longer we let something fester, the more likely it will become toxic.

And finally, it's imperative you confess your sin before God and others on a regular basis.[95] It's impossible to be contrite and hard-hearted at the same time. Confession is good for the soul, and it's good for your relationships too. So, when you've blown it, own it. In fact, here are the six most powerful words in every relationship: *I was wrong. Please forgive me.*

Hundreds of times, I've seen relationships blow up and end—not because God was unable to rescue them, but because people were unwilling to get help early in their struggles. If you're seriously ill, you go to the doctor. If you need a mortgage loan, you go to a loan officer. If you need to get in shape, you go to a trainer at the gym. Why do we wait to get relational and marriage help from a professional when we need it? Support is available, but you need to humble yourself and ask for it.

---

93 James 4:6.

94 James 1:19–21.

95 James 5:16.

HOPE REMAINS

For many of you, this is a difficult and painful chapter to read. Some because you are still horribly wounded. Others because you were the one doing the wounding.

Believe me when I say I understand. By no means am I trying to stir up more emotional turmoil for you. However, it's nearly impossible to write about hope and ignore one of the great hope robbers of our time.

The stories of divorce are common. The pain is real and tragic. God hates divorce because it leaves His kids a bloody mess. One indeed is the loneliest number, especially when you were one with another human and now you are not.

My heart aches for you because divorce lingers in our souls for a long time. Sometimes it makes you extremely angry. At other times, terribly sad. I know. I have sat in my office many times and wept with those who weep.

All that being said—and this is important, so you need to hear me say it loud and clear— divorce is *not* the unpardonable sin. If you have children, you probably will never be entirely out of the other person's life, but there is life after divorce.

God is not done with you.

He has not abandoned you.

As any father would, Father God aches for you and with you.

And as I have written already (but it's worth repeating often), God's specialty is redemption, restoration, and renewal. If you're divorced, it's likely too late for your previous marriage, but it's never too late for you to personally know and experience God's healing touch in your life.

My momma went through a divorce. She endured years of emotional abuse and unfaithfulness by my dad. He broke her heart. She was embarrassed and felt a lot of guilt and shame even though she put up with far more than most would have done in her situation and for far longer than anyone else I've met. After the divorce, she wondered if she would spend the rest of her life alone.

Then, one day, God brought an exceptional man named Frank Mayo into her life. A godly man. A humble man. A man who loved her (and her kids) for over twenty-five years until he went to be with the Lord. My mom used to tell me, "When I was hopeless, God brought a Boaz into my world."[96] He sure did.

God had a plan of restoration for my mom.

She was never beyond God's healing power.

You're never beyond God's hope, either. Never.

That's what makes uncommon hope so astonishing.

---

96 Find the story of Ruth and Boaz in the book of Ruth.

EPIC STEPS

- Where have you seen a miracle in your life or the life of another because God was in the mix? Make a list of those experiences and use this listing of God moments to remind yourself of His faithfulness. Uncommon hope is often discovered when we remember the uncommon goodness of God.

- Where have you given up hope in your marriage? How would a change in your perspective, and getting help from a good Christian counselor, perhaps improve your marriage? Are you keeping "short accounts" and confessing your sins to God and others as needed? If not, why? What's holding you back?

FOURTEEN

INFERTILITY, MISCARRIAGE, AND OTHER LOSS

In my deepest wound I saw your glory, and it dazzled me.
—St. Augustine

In most books, there are chapters an author doesn't want to write. This is that chapter for me.

My daughter, Jessica Marie, turned forty-one this year. I have another daughter, Michelle, who is thirty-five. (Yes, I became a dad when I was seven-ish.) I love both of my girls. I would do anything for them. Of course, my two boys are special too, but there truly is something about a father and his daughters.

Both my girls are incredible with kids. From the time Jessica was little, if you asked her what she wanted to be when she grew up, she would say, "A mommy!" Michelle was not quite as fixated on motherhood, but she, too, dreams of having children of her own someday.

Sadly, however, Jessica is infertile. She was pregnant once for a very brief time, but that pregnancy ended in a miscarriage. My heart aches for her so much, but there is nothing I can do to make this go away.

Of course, I have prayed. I have begged God to open her womb. I've bargained with God too. For years, I prayed, "God, whatever you want from me, I'll give you. Just give my daughter a baby!" And month after month, year after year, nothing happened. Nothing but pain.

By the way, please don't email or write to me and say, "You or your daughter just needed more faith!" Fair question: How is that statement truly helpful to anyone in a moment of hopelessness?

Somewhere, somehow, somebody decided to define faith as something that is more about you and me and what *we* do than all about God. So, when someone says, "You need more faith, BROTHA!" what that apparently means is I need to have more, be more, or do more.

Seriously?

I didn't get saved because of something I accomplished, and I don't get anything from God because of what I can do. It's never been about you or me.

On my best day, I might be a six or seven out of ten as a Christ follower (and those days are few and far between). God doesn't ever look at my life and think, *Whoa, look at that Bubna guy! He's amazing! I think he deserves a miracle or two. Gabriel, next time he asks for something, let's be sure to give him what he deserves.*

Nope.

Never.

Not gonna happen that way.

Everything good in my life is because God is good. It's always an act of unmerited favor.

That's why faith, biblical faith, is not about me, either. It's not about what I can muster. It's not about what I can do. Faith is always and ever about God. Period.

Yeah, but . . .

The TV preacher said my faith is the key to getting my miracle from God. I just need to "name it and claim it," and it'll be mine!

I read in a best-selling book that "miracles are the fruits of my faith!"

I went to a healing crusade, and the preacher said I need to "create my own miracle!"

Here's why I get so frustrated by all of this religious hoopla: because faith *does* matter. However, it's not the *measure* of my faith; it's the *object* of my faith that matters. It is Who I look to, Who I turn to, and Who I trust in that determines what does or doesn't happen.

Without question, faith is important. Faith invites the miracle-working intervention of God into a situation that seems hopeless. Faith is necessary. But it's not faith in faith or even faith in my ability to have faith—it's faith *in God*.

And faith in God means He's the miracle-worker, not me.

He is the source of anything and everything good that might happen, not me.

I don't ever create my own miracle or force God into action because I've declared and claimed my miracle in JEEEEEEsus's name! All I can do is cry out to Him and choose to believe more in Him, not more in me.

In other words, when God sees a pathetic and desperate human (like you or me) choose to put his or her hope in an almighty God, that is having faith "in God," and that connects us to the divine. Faith is throwing myself wholeheartedly on God's mercy and goodness while crying, "Lord, if you don't do something here, nothing great will ever happen. I believe in you, Jesus! Help me despite my unbelief!"

IT'S NOT ABOUT ME (OR YOU)

Believing in my power to change something at a miraculous level is silly. Except for the transforming power of God working in and through me, there is nothing I can do. However, when I place my faith *in Him* because of the relationship and trust I have *in Him*, nothing is impossible.

When Jesus scolded the disciples for their "lack of faith" in the middle of a storm, He confronted them with the fact that they weren't fixing their hope and faith on Him. "Why are you afraid and having such an itsy-bitsy faith in me? Watch what happens when I speak to the wind and the waves. As long as you're with me, you're safe!" [97]

When Jesus challenged His disciples to seek the kingdom of God above all else and not to worry about material provision, He said, "God takes care of everything, even the grass of the field and the birds of the air! Why do you have such little faith in His goodness?"[98] Jesus pointed people to the kindness and faithfulness of the Father, and He wanted them to have faith in Him.

When Peter got out of the boat, he walked on water for a bit. But when he started to sink, and Jesus reached out for Peter, Jesus said, "Pete, your faith in Me is too small. Why did you doubt me?"[99] Peter's problem is our problem. We take our eyes off Jesus, and we not only look at the storms around us, but we think, *Who am I? I can't walk on water!*

We doubt our Savior.

Of course, we can't walk on water.

But with Jesus, we can.

It's always about Him.

Jesus calms the storm, not me.

God ultimately provides for my needs, not me.

Water-walking miracles happen when I stay focused on Jesus and His power, *not mine.*

It's not the size of my faith that matters; it's what I believe about the size of my God. (You might want to read that last line again.)

The more I know, trust, believe in, and hope in a great big God, great big things can happen. That's why Jesus told His disciples that faith as small as a mustard seed can move mountains! (Did you know that a mustard seed is about the size of a pinhead? That's awfully small!)

That "mustard seed" statement of Jesus makes absolutely no sense

---

97 Matthew 8:26 (Bubna Paraphrase).

98 Matthew 6:28-34 (Bubna Paraphrase)

99 Matthew 14:31 (Bubna Paraphrase)

unless we see His point. Jesus is saying nothing is impossible for the person who hopes in God. It's not about a mountain of faith somehow resident in me; it's about a little bit of faith put in a mountain of a God!

"But, Kurt, the writer of Hebrews said that 'faith is confidence in what we hope for and assurance about what we do not see.'[100] He says, 'we' so doesn't that mean it's about me?"

Yes, the writer defined faith, but the entire "faith in action" chapter of Hebrews 11 lists person after person who became legends of faith because they trusted and hoped in God, not in their ability to have a ton of faith.

We must zoom out to see in context all the New Testament teaches about faith. When we have a biblical and broader perspective, it helps us understand that the "what" in Hebrews 11:1 is really a "Who."

That verse could just as easily read: "Faith is confidence in *Who* we hope for (God) and assurance of *Who* we do not see (God)."

When we make it about the "what" (us and our level of faith) versus the Who, we tend to make it about us, not Him, and that's never encouraged in the Word. Jesus said, "All things are possible with God."[101]

I'm sorry if you've been told differently, but these men and women of faith in Hebrews never put their hope in *their* abilities or *their* wisdom or *their* strength or even *their* faith. From Abel to Rahab, God was the hero of their stories.

God was the one who opened the womb of Sarah.

He was the one who spared the life of Moses.

Jehovah was the one who opened the Red Sea and brought down the walls of Jericho.

These great people were great because they put their hope in God. Don't overlook or discount those two incredibly important words—*in God.*

---

100 Hebrews 11:1 (NIV).

101 Mark 10:27 (NIV).

PAINFUL WORDS

When someone you know experiences traumatic and unexpected loss, and they're grieving, please don't pat them on the back and say, "You just need more faith, and everything will be okay." The pain that misguided and self-righteous statement can bring to someone in the midst of loss and grief is cruel, not helpful.

I mentioned the loss of my first grandson, Phineas, in chapter one. As confessed, the months that followed that loss left me spiritually and emotionally bleeding. I had (and still have) more questions than answers. I don't know why we went through that devastating experience. I have no idea why some children are born to drug addicts, and they're normal, and why some are born to health nuts (like my daughter-in-law), and they die.

What I do know is how injurious it was when well-meaning people said things such as:

"Well, at least he's in a better place."

"I'm sorry for your loss, but your loss is heaven's gain."

"What do you think Jesus is trying to teach you through all of this? I'm praying you will have more faith." (Implying my lack of faith regarding Phineas was at least, in part, responsible for what happened to him.)

Each statement, even though they were made by people who love me, cast me deeper and deeper into despair.

WEEP AND SAY NOTHING

Probably, because people are uncomfortable and they don't know what to say, they say the first dumb thing that comes into their heads. They don't mean to be mean. They're not attempting to make someone's pain worse. But they do.

Can I suggest a better way?

It's okay—in fact, it's good—to weep with those who weep and to mourn with those who mourn.[102] The best thing you can do for someone who's bleeding out emotionally is to wrap your arms around them and wail. Loudly. Often. Much.

I fear in our culture people tend to land in one of two unhelpful places. First, there's the Tony Robbins Mr. Positive person who wants to help us overcome our crisis by "unlocking the power of positive thinking!" The other group includes the "faith masters" who tell us to overcome our sorrow by "exercising our faith muscle."

Listen, being positive is always better than being negative, and as previously stated, faith does matter. However, the best thing you can do for someone you love who's hurting is to feel their pain and hurt with them.

One of my best friends, a guy named Tim Gump (no relation to Forrest), would sit and listen to me for hours over coffee at Starbucks after the loss of my grandson. He just listened. He cried. He bled with me and wept with me. He never offered any superficial clichés or spiritual platitudes. For weeks, he was my supporting and caring friend. A friend who felt my pain and mourned with me. I would give Tim one of my kidneys if he needed it. Maybe both.

I DO HAVE HOPE, BUT I STILL STRUGGLE

When you lose someone you love, whether they go quickly, slowly, or unexpectedly, it's normal to ache. Walking in uncommon hope does not mean living without grief.

Over the past twenty years, I've lost a dad, a stepdad, a father-in-law, two valued mentors, and several dear friends. Loss hurts. Every Father's Day, I ache a bit knowing all my fathers are gone. When I get stuck in life or ministry, my first thought is to call my uncle Don (one of the mentors I miss), but there's no cell service in heaven.

Someone once asked me, "Is it all right to grieve?" I said,

---

102 Romans 12:15.

"Absolutely. Cry. Weep. Wail. Maybe even curse a little, but don't grieve as those who have no hope."

In the book of First Corinthians, Paul writes in chapter fifteen about the resurrection. He offers the Corinthians hope by reminding them that because Jesus rose from the dead, death no longer has the last say with us. He declares death is "swallowed up in victory" because Jesus defeated death.[103] That's a hope I can hang onto, and it gives me peace.

To the believers in another city, Paul says, "Brothers and sisters, we do not want you to be uninformed about those who sleep in death, so that you do not grieve like the rest of mankind, who have no hope." And then he asks them to encourage one another with the truth of our eventual resurrection.[104]

Paul didn't say, "Don't grieve." He didn't say, "Get over it, and have more faith!" But he did say, "Don't get stuck in your grief because you think death is the end of your story. It's not." The death of someone we love will always include pain, but it doesn't have to include hopelessness. I can't remember where I read it, but the late Billy Graham once said, "You're born. You suffer. You die. But fortunately, there's a loophole."

I long for the day when I will be reunited with my family and friends. I desire, more than I can express, to experience an eternity in which God Himself will "wipe every tear from our eyes. There will be no more death or mourning or crying or pain."[105]

I sometimes dream about playing with Phineas in the sand on the beaches of the new heaven and new earth to come. Death without the hope of the resurrection would be agonizing. On this side of eternity, our loss feels unbearable. I know. But this side of eternity isn't all there is for you or me.

We'll be together soon, Phin.

---

103 1 Corinthians 15:54–55.

104 1 Thessalonians 4:13–18.

105 Revelation 21:4 (NIV).

EPIC STEPS

- Have you ever been wounded by someone who told you that you just needed more faith in God? Have you forgiven that person? Note: Sometimes we need to forgive them more than once. If there's still raw pain in your soul, then forgive them again (seventy times seven if necessary).[106]

- Check out this amazing article for some very practical steps you can take to love on someone who has experienced great loss:

  https://medium.com/@shaylaleeraquel/grief-etiquette-for-the-unenlightened-941dd4a97be

- Ask someone you know who is in pain and grieving, "What can I do or say that will help and not hurt you in this situation?" Then please do that. Now.

---

106 Matthew 18:22.

FIFTEEN

BUCK NAKED!

Jesus wants something for you, not from you.

—*Anonymous*

F ew things throw people into a tailspin of depression faster than money issues—more specifically, the lack of money. A bad marriage or a wandering child (which I'll cover in the next chapter) messes with us emotionally. But struggling week after week or year after year in financial turmoil can leave us feeling like hopeless losers. We feel buck naked (i.e., without money), and it's discouraging.

If, by chance, you are independently wealthy, or you've never struggled with your finances, you can skip this chapter. If not, please keep reading.

Before I go on, I promise you this won't be a chapter that beats you up. My intent is not to cause guilt or shame. I do, however, want to give you some helpful and very practical information you can use to move toward financial freedom, hope, and health. I've never been accused of being very profound, but I am practical; so, let's get real.

It's estimated about 80 percent of Americans are living paycheck to paycheck.[107] That means most of us have too much *month* left at the

---

107 Emmie Martin, Make It, "The Government Shutdown Spotlights a Bigger Issue: 78% of US Workers Live Paycheck to Paycheck," last updated January 10, 2019, https://www.cnbc.com/2019/01/09/shutdown-highlights-that-4-in-5-us-workers-live-paycheck-to-paycheck.html.

end of the *money*! Money is fun if you've got some, and not so much fun if you don't.

I know. I've been there.

BUSTED AND BANKRUPT

Back in my twenties, I made some horrible financial decisions. In fact, I didn't make just one or two dumb choices; I made a whole boatload of them.

Once upon a time, in a far, faraway place called Florida, I got the brilliant idea to buy an RV. Everybody needs one—or so I thought. They are enjoyable and great for the fam. There is nothing wrong with owning some fun-on-wheels. However, being able to afford it and make the payments is generally a good idea.

My wife kindly asked two very important questions. First, why do we need this? And second, how are we going to pay for it?

"Why do we need this?" I reacted. "You're kidding, right? Besides, I make plenty of money."

Here was my profound reasoning (and trust me, I can rationalize just about anything): We were about to move from Florida back to Southern California. We had four kids, a new Rottweiler puppy, a cat, several pet rodents, and an assortment of other creatures too numerous to mention. What better way to travel three thousand miles than in the comfort of our home away from home? It would be like our very own ark. Plus, we would save lots of money by not needing to stay in motels or eat in restaurants.

It seemed like a brilliant—no—*perfect* idea.

In case you're curious, that plan didn't work out so well. Our RV was a converted van. It barely slept two comfortably, let alone two adults and four kids. Now imagine driving for five days with four fighting kids, an incontinent puppy, and a cat trying really hard to get to the pet rats. It was a nightmare. I might be exaggerating a bit about the animals, but you get the picture.

When we (and by *we,* I mean *me)* bought the RV, I was making pretty good money working in Florida. My first big mistake was assuming I would have no problem finding a well-paying job right away when we landed back in California. After all, I was young, talented, and in possession of a very impressive résumé.

What I didn't know was the business market and economy were tanking in Southern California. In fact, it was one of those rare times in California when homes were depreciating. And during that time, thousands and thousands of people were being laid off. Businesses were downsizing like crazy.

I called everybody I knew. I was willing to drive hours one-way to work if need be. I sent out more than fifty letters and knocked on a bunch of doors. Nothing. No work anywhere. We went through our savings faster than a rat goes through a Cheeto.

You can imagine how excited I was to be making an RV payment every month. Laura's question, "And how are we going to pay for this?" haunted me.

I finally got a job completely outside of my field of experience as a loan officer at a local bank. It was commission only and didn't offer any health benefits for ninety days.

Why is it you pay through the nose for health insurance all your life and never really need it until you don't have it?

One morning, my youngest son, Isaac, woke up, got out of bed, and collapsed with a scream of pain. He was five years old, and we had always thought he was pretty much indestructible. That kid had the highest pain tolerance of any boy I've ever seen. Sometimes, as a little tyke, he would fall hard, get up, shrug it off, and just keep on going without so much as a peep. When we heard him wailing from his bedroom, we knew it was something serious, so we took him to our pediatrician.

The doctor, whom we couldn't afford, sent us to the emergency room, which we couldn't afford. The ER doctor ran some tests, which we couldn't afford, and then admitted our son for more tests, which we couldn't afford. The diagnosis ended up being very serious. Isaac had a rare form of bone infection (osteomyelitis), which might require weeks of hospitalization, and which—you guessed it—we couldn't afford. I figured I was going to have to sell a kidney or something to pay for everything. I remember thinking, *God, what are you doing to me? I tithe faithfully. I serve you. I'm doing my best here. But I'm going bankrupt. What's up?*

I've discovered asking God "What's up?" is generally one of those questions He answers pretty clearly, especially when we need correction. As you may have noticed by now, I am exceptionally skilled at blame-shifting and denial. I do not like taking responsibility. I would rather blame God, or my dad, or my wife, or my dog, or somebody else—anybody else.

Thankfully, God healed Isaac (you can find that story in *Epic Grace*, my first book), and he was discharged without having to spend weeks in the hospital. But here's the gist of what God taught me during my time of financial and emotional despair: Providing for my every need is God's job; managing with wisdom what I have is mine.

I now take full responsibility for my stupid mistakes. I was a financial idiot. But honestly, no one ever taught me how to manage my finances. That's why I'm writing this chapter—to give you some hope and teach you some valuable and important lessons I learned the hard way.

STRUGGLE IS NORMAL

Nobody likes to struggle. No one wakes up in the morning and prays, "God, please give me more trials today!" On the contrary, we humans tend to avoid it at all costs. But everybody struggles with something and most struggle with money. I've never met a person who hasn't made at least one major financial blunder in his or her life, and I know lots of people who've made plenty.

Even if you haven't made a ton of mistakes, the majority of Americans are living hand-to-mouth. So, if you're worried about paying your bills or saving enough money for retirement or your kids' college education, then you're normal. Welcome to the club.

I had a conversation several years ago with a guy who was depressed and embarrassed about the state of his finances. As we talked, he wouldn't make eye contact with me he felt so ashamed. I told him what I'm telling you: "Yes, you've made some huge mistakes, but you're in good company. So don't beat yourself up or let the enemy beat you up, either. God's grace and mercy extend to our finances."

You see, when we get focused on our mistakes, we lose hope, withdraw from God, and isolate from others who can help us. I am not making light of your bad decisions. I am not saying it's no big deal. I'm just saying it's always better to bring our failures to the light and to get help rather than cower in the darkness of shame.

I love the practical wisdom found in James 5:16 (NLT): "Confess your sins to each other and pray for each other so that you may be healed." Notice here, James does not say, "*If* you have sin in your life, confess it." He assumes we all do (because we all do). So James says here's the path to healing: Confess your sins.

I want you to admit your financial mistakes, because until you do, you won't reach out to get the help you desperately need. Decide now to stop hiding in shame and to get real with people.

- Ask for help from someone who is good with his or her finances.

- See a credit counselor.

- Sign up to attend a financial seminar such as Financial Peace University.[108]

---

108 Find out more at www.daveramsey.com.

CHANGE YOUR BELIEFS, CHANGE YOUR LIFE

Struggling is sometimes the result of our false beliefs and poor behaviors. Shame is never productive, so I'm not making that statement to make you feel worse than you already do. But to get better and to get healthy, you probably need to change what you think about money. What you believe always affects what you do.

The following was my pattern of thinking and operating for years. See if you recognize any of this in yourself.

- I confused desire with need, and I could easily rationalize what I wanted. (I bought the RV thinking it would save us money.)

- I believed the cultural lie that more, new, and bigger is always better. Did you know commercials are designed to make you wallow in discontentment? They feed the myth, *I want, I need, I must have!*

- I can afford my credit limit, and I'll pay off my debt easily and quickly! We reason, *My bank wouldn't give me a $10,000 credit limit if I weren't good for it, right?!* Wrong. Your bank doesn't care about you; they care only about making money.

King Solomon, who wrote the book of Proverbs, once said, "Good planning and hard work lead to prosperity, but hasty shortcuts lead to poverty. Those who love pleasure become poor; those who love wine and luxury will never be rich."[109] He was correct then and now. A hasty shortcut (like using a credit card and living beyond your means) can lead to trouble. Loving pleasure—like "needing" the newest iPhone—can lead to poverty.

Our culture and Madison Street marketing tell us going into debt

---

109 Proverbs 21:5, 17 (NLT).

is okay and something everybody does. We think it's something we must do to be happy. The truth is, I've never met anybody who was financially healthy because of their cash-back points.

Here's another false belief: the idea that more money will fix all my problems. More often than not, however, my problem wasn't due to the amount of money I had or didn't have but to the way I managed my resources. Believe it or not (and I hope you believe it), money isn't the cure-all. If you're bad at managing $2,000 a month, you'll probably be lousy at managing $20,000 a month.

How many times have you heard or read about some celebrity who makes a gazillion bucks a year and then blows it all? I read some time ago about a young sports star who made over ten million dollars a year (that's like $200,000 a *week* and $27,000 a day!). He had the multimillion-dollar house on the beach and the fast and expensive cars until he blew his knee out, and in less than four years, he lost it all.

You see, it's not just about what you make but how you manage what you make. For most of us, the problem isn't a lack of money but the fact that we believe the wrong things and so we do the wrong things. I know that might seem a bit harsh, but your financial wholeness will not happen while you're in denial and refuse to change your ways.

WALLOW OR GROW!

Here's some good news: Your pain, your struggles, and even your mistakes can be a good teacher if you'll let God use them to get you back on track.

Rather than wallow in your pain, deny your pain, or blame others for your pain, let it be your teacher. The writer of Hebrews made this clear: "No discipline is enjoyable while it is happening—it's painful! But afterward there will be a peaceful harvest of right living for those who are trained in this way."[110] The biblical principle here is clear: Pain

---

110 Hebrews 12:11 (NLT).

can lead to gain. God can use it in your life, but only if you let it show you where you've gone sideways. Let your mistakes point you back to God and His ways.

I've got a buddy who has filed bankruptcy three times in his life. He digs himself into a hole and then bails on his financial responsibilities. There are two terribly sad things about this guy. First, he was completely unbothered by his actions. He figured the corporations left holding the bag could afford it. And the second thing that's unfortunate is he hasn't learned from his past mistakes. What's worse, his financial actions have also cost him two marriages.

By now, you've figured out I feel strongly about this reality: We all make mistakes. We all have failed financially at least once. But God's plan is for us to *grow* through our struggles, not just *go* through them. Growth starts with a change in our beliefs, which leads to a change in our behavior. Remember, you are never hopeless when God is in the mix.

MORE BANG FOR YOUR BUCK!

Okay, debt is a genuine problem, but I want to shift gears now and focus on how to manage what we do have with more wisdom.

Like I wrote earlier, in my early twenties, I was ignorant about how to manage money. Most of the decisions I made about spending money were based either on how much I had in my checking account or how much available credit I still had left on a credit card. (If you looked up *impulse buyer* in the dictionary, you would find my picture right next to the definition.) I had no financial plan, no operational budget, and absolutely no way of tracking whether I could actually afford what I was buying.

Out of desperation one day, I asked my very wise stepdad to help me, and he did. What I'm passing along is what I learned from him, and it's a smart approach to managing your finances.

First, live within your means and decide to act your wage.[111] I have confessed my stupidity to you, so I'm not casting stones at anyone. But you won't and can't get healthy until you decide to live on *less* than you make rather than *more* than you earn. It's not wise, and in fact, dangerously foolish for individuals, families, or governments to spend more than they generate.

As I write this, the American national debt is over twenty-one trillion dollars and growing. As a country, we are not living within our means, and it will lead to disaster at some point in the future.

Once again, the wisdom of Solomon addresses living beyond our means. He wrote, "The best food and olive oil are stored up in the houses of wise people. But a foolish man eats up everything he has."[112] In other words, a wise person stores up for the future, but the foolish person gobbles up everything, and then some.

The money runs out if we are spending it faster than we make it! I know, brilliant insight, huh? But something we choose to ignore too often. Unless we exercise restraint, sooner or later the credit stops, and our house of credit cards comes falling down.

We must first decide to stop using money we don't have in our bank account. It's not easy, but nothing changes until we do. It's basic math; there must be more pluses than minuses for us to ever get ahead.

We also must recognize the difference between a need and a want. Honestly, there are very few things we actually need. The apostle Paul wrote, "If we have food and clothing, we will be content with that."[113] It sounds as if food, clothing, and perhaps a roof over our head is enough. But we live in a culture that constantly feeds in us what I call the want machine.

- *Buy it NOW and pay NO INTEREST until 2025!*

---

111 A well-known Dave Ramsey quote from his Financial Peace University (FPU) course.

112 Proverbs 21:20 (NIRV).

113 1 Timothy 6:8 (NIV).

- *For JUST $199 per month and zero down, you can drive a brand-new car today!*

- *This deal is ONLY good for 24 hours, and then the price goes up! FOREVER!* (Never mind you might be paying for it forever too.)

We see something we like, we want it, and so we get it—now. Whether we can afford it or not. It's the American way, and it's killing us. In fact, the idea of delayed gratification seems absurd to many. The word *restraint* is considered almost a four-letter word in our society. If it feels good, do it! If it looks good, buy it! And every time we do, we go a little farther into a hole that's becoming harder and harder to escape.

Here's the alternative: Learn to be content and practice restraint. Then trust God to provide for your legitimate needs. A wise person learns to live within their means.

The second step in getting financially healthy is to reduce and then eliminate your debt as soon as possible. Once you stop adding to the debt monkey on your back, then you can begin to chip away at it. You can't get out of a hole while you're continuing to dig deeper. But after you put the "credit shovel" down, you can begin the path to financial freedom by getting out of debt.

Imagine what your life would be like if you were completely debt-free. What might you be able to do someday if you were able to put the hundreds of dollars you spend on credit card debt and interest into a savings account? What would your life be like if you had no payments?

What might you be able to do for others or the kingdom of God if you were completely free of debt?

The motivational speaker and author, Zig Ziglar, once said, "If you do the things you need to do when you need to do them, then someday you can do the things you want to do when you want to do them!"

Debt enslaves us because "the borrower is the slave of the lender."[114] It traps us, and it wraps us in a web of stress, fear, and frustration. It also robs us of the joy of generosity. It steals our hope for a truly better future.

I spoke with a guy some time ago who had over twenty credit cards. He was almost maxed out on every one of them because he was using credit card cash advances to pay his monthly credit card bills. He was losing sleep and chunks of his hair. He was thirty-six, had a beautiful home, a beautiful wife, and three beautiful kids, but there was no joy in his life. When he came to me, he was seriously contemplating running away to South America because he couldn't see any other way out.

Instead of him bolting, we worked out a plan together. First, we cut up all of his credit cards. Yes, radical surgery, but necessary. Then we put into place what Dave Ramsey calls (in the Financial Peace University course) the debt payoff snowball.

Here's the idea in a nutshell:

- You list your debts in order—the smallest to the largest balance.

- Then, concentrate on the smallest one. Make minimum payments on everything else, but pay more than the minimum due on the smallest one to pay it off as quickly as possible. (The concept here is to knock off some of your debt rapidly so you'll have some quick wins!)

- After you pay off the first debt on the list, you take all the money you were applying to it and move it to the next one on the list.

(That's why it's a snowball. As the snowball rolls over, it picks up more snow!)

Honestly, it took my friend years to get completely out of debt.

---

114 Proverbs 22:7 (ESV).

He also had to take a second, part-time job and sell a bunch of stuff he once thought he needed but didn't.

I'll be painfully clear: You can't get ahead by staying a slave to debt.

Let's briefly look at the third thing you need to do to get more bang for your buck: You need to tell your money where to go, or it just goes!

There are two critical components needed to discover and maintain financial health: a budget and a usable financial tracking system.

What's the purpose of a budget? A budget identifies what you make and your current expenses. It lists all of your income and all of your obligations. When my stepdad helped me put together my very first budget, I was making pretty good money. However, I had no idea what my monthly expenses were. I didn't know how much we spent on groceries each month. I didn't know how much my average utility bills were. I was clueless about how much we spent on clothes, entertainment, miscellaneous stuff, and I was shocked when I figured that out.

A budget is a plan that accurately describes what you have in resources and where you need to apply those resources. Imagine my dismay at discovering I was consistently spending more—way more—than I was making in a month.

A good plan begins with a good budget, but too many people stop there. People take the time to figure out what they have and what they need but then do nothing to monitor or track how they're doing each month. That's why you need to find or create a usable system for monitoring your expenses versus your income. (Something like QuickBooks, Quicken, Moneydance, or an old-fashioned column ledger will do!)

A budget is one-half of the financial system you need to keep you out of trouble. The other half is a simple and doable way to keep track of how you're doing compared to your budget.

Find something.

Use something.

Do something.

Today.

There is so much more I could write here, but let me finish with one last gem of wisdom from the book of Proverbs. "A house is built by wisdom and becomes strong through good sense. Through knowledge its rooms are filled with all sorts of precious riches and valuables."[115]

God's plan is for *your* house (including your finances) to be built by wisdom and made strong through good sense. It's an incredible way to live in uncommon hope and the best way to experience God's epic plan. Getting there will take time, hard work, and some help, but it's worth it and hope will return.

---

115 Proverbs 24:3–4 (NLT).

EPIC STEPS

- How have you bought into the view of our culture that promotes living beyond your means? Heart check: If you're living paycheck to paycheck, or you're unable to pay off your credit card balance in full each month, that's a pretty good indication that something must change.

- Find a local Financial Peace University (FPU) course by Dave Ramsey and sign up for it today. Even if you think you're doing okay with your finances, the investment you make in this course will pay back in huge dividends.

SIXTEEN

THE CHALLENGE OF INFLUENCING CHILDREN WITH HOPE

God loves the worst person in His world more than you love the best person in yours. He loves everybody more than you love anybody.
—*John Ortberg*

Parenting is a challenge. It doesn't matter what your education or experience might be when it comes to kids; we're all in the same boat: continually learning.

By the way, even if you're not a parent yet, you probably do have influence in the life of a child and a parent. Please see the value you have and the contribution you can make that can foster hope in others, and read on.

There are many helpful books about raising kids. I've probably read at least thirty of them (no kidding). When you become a parent, you realize how much you thought you knew about children when, in fact, you know almost nothing.

When my first child, Jessica, was born, it didn't take me long to figure out I had no idea what I was doing.

I'd never changed a diaper.

I'd never cleaned a freshly cut umbilical cord. (Gross.)

I'd never dressed an infant.

I'd never treated diaper rash.

I'd never tried to comfort a kid with colic, and that's nearly impossible.

I knew babies needed food, and that's about it, but since that came from Momma, I was off the hook.

Nonetheless, I learned. I grew. Eventually, after a few months, I remember thinking, *I've got this. Piece of cake. No big deal.*

Then Jessica started crawling, and by nine months of age, she was walking. (Yes, all my children are very advanced.) Keeping tabs on a wandering infant—without the use of enormous amounts of duct tape—isn't easy. In the rare moments when my wife left me home alone with Jessica, I felt like I was chasing a pinball, but I was the one getting whacked at every turn.

"NO! Don't touch that!"

"STOP! You can't put the ducky in the toilet!"

"Those are Daddy's precious and priceless toys, NOT yours. Please leave them alone!"

I'm pretty sure she couldn't understand my words. (She wasn't *that* advanced.) But I know she understood my tone and body language, and yet it didn't seem to matter. An hour with her made me a little crazy and dead-dog exhausted. I often would say to my Wonder Woman wife, "How do you do this all day?" and I usually just got a look from her that said, "Don't ask!"

IS THERE A RETURN POLICY?

When Jessica hit the "terrific twos," it went from challenging to unbelievably tough. I'm choosing to be kind here, but two was pretty terrible for us. My daughter was so stubborn, independent, and strong-willed (just like her Irish mother) that at one point, I asked my wife if there was a return policy.

Unfortunately, about the time we thought we had Jessica and parenting under control, she'd change. It's weird how kids keep growing and changing when you feed them.

When my wife told me she was pregnant with our second child, I was both thrilled and terrified. I reasoned, "If number two turns out as difficult and demanding as number one, we're doomed!" I was feeling hopeless about our chances of survival.

I wish I could tell you raising a strong-willed child made our marriage stronger. I wish I could tell you struggling with Jessica drew Laura and me closer. It didn't.

Our frustration and exhaustion made us both grumpy. We made Winnie's friend, Eeyore, look like a ray of sunshine. You can't or shouldn't be mean to a child, but it's easy to be mean to your spouse when you can't take it out on your toddler. I remember coming home from work one night and Laura met me at the door. I hadn't taken off my coat or set down my briefcase when she almost threw Jessica into my arms and said, "You deal with her now! I'm done for the day!" On another unhappy note, and what made things worse for me, was how infrequently we had sex. I was more than a little surprised about how Laura got pregnant again.

Thankfully, God answered my prayers, and Nathan, our second child, was the mellowest, happiest, and easiest kid born in the twentieth century! We'd sometimes sit him down in the living room with some toys, and he was content to sit there and play quietly by himself for an hour. In fact, I sometimes wondered if Nate was okay or if he had a brain disability. It turns out he was fine. Nathan graduated as valedictorian from his high school and *cum laude* from college. He was just quiet and easy and the exact opposite of his mischievous sister.

SAME BUT DIFFERENT

If you have more than one child, you already know this: No two kids are the same. Yes, same home, same parents, but different. We had four, and they were all unique. The good news is that makes each one of them special. The less-than-good news is you never get to the point—and I mean, *never*—when you truly have this parenting thing all figured out.

Because each kid is different and each child constantly changes, you never get a break from learning more about becoming a good parent. Infants become toddlers. Toddlers become little people (who want to rule your world). And little people become preadolescents, who become teenagers, who become young adults, who become independent, self-sufficient adults (until they move back home at thirty). And with each new developmental stage and every new child added to your family, there are a lot of changes.

I'll write about how to deal with the "C" word (i.e., change) in the next chapter. However, my point here is crucial for you to understand: You always will be learning as a parent because nothing about your family is ever static. Kids change. You change. The family dynamic changes.

So don't fight it.

Don't be discouraged.

Don't give up on your kid or yourself, either.

And please don't beat up yourself (or your kid).

It'll be okay.

Hope is there for those who choose *not* to see their kid, themselves, or their family as hopeless.

Once, after a painful and emotional encounter with Jessica as a thirteen-year-old, I told her, "I've never been the parent of a teenager! And you've never been a teenager before! So, let's give each other some room to grow." She did. I did. She survived. We survived. In fact, I'm very proud of her today, and we're extremely close.

The best thing Laura and I did was to get some help. We read as much as we could about how to raise kids without killing them or each other. We also turned to some wise and experienced friends who told us what I'm telling you. "Welcome to parenting. You'll be fine. Stay the course. Be consistent. Don't give up. Someday, you'll be proud." And Laura and I are both fine and proud today.

Parenting was never easy for us, and we made plenty of mistakes, but family is the best place to learn how to be patient, how to extend grace to one another, and how to forgive. I love what my friend Lori Wildenberg says: "The parenting adventure is a messy one. Like so much of parenting, we don't know what it will be like until we are there."[116]

WHAT ABOUT WHEN THINGS GO WRONG?

About now, some of you are thinking, *I'm glad you didn't kill anyone in the process and good for you that your kids turned out okay, but mine didn't! My child is broken, far from God, I'm not proud, and my kid won't even talk to me. What the Hades am I supposed to do now?*

Believe me when I tell you, I understand. Our kids haven't always made the best choices, and we've agonized at times over their decisions. They're all adults now, and we've been empty nesters for a long time, but out of the house doesn't mean out of your heart. We still worry sometimes. We still get frustrated. We've watched our adult children make choices that are painful for us. In some ways, being a parent is tougher now because we have all the same concerns but utterly no control. I can't threaten to ground them or to take away their car keys anymore! If anybody ever tells you, "Oh, just give it time, and when they're on their own, it'll be much easier," they're either lying, or they're idiots.

Next to being a good spouse, being a good parent is the toughest job you'll ever have in life, and that role never stops. Parenting is a lifetime responsibility. You can't divorce your kids. Nevertheless, don't give up; hope is always within reach, so keep reading.

---

116 Lori Wildenberg, *The Messy Life of Parenting: Powerful and Practical Ways to Strengthen Family Connections* (Birmingham, AL: New Hope Publishers, 2018).

PRODIGAL PROBLEMS

As a pastor, I've sat with many parents over the years who have a prodigal son or daughter, and they are discouraged. They go through something similar to the five stages of grief described by the American psychiatrist, Elisabeth Kübler-Ross: denial, anger, bargaining, depression, and acceptance.

For a season, maybe weeks or months, it's easier to ignore or deny there's any problem with your son or daughter. One day, however, the reality of the situation smacks you in the face, and you get angry with them and probably mad at yourself. You try to bargain with your kid, and when that fails, you attempt to bargain with God. "Jesus, if you get my kid out of this, I'll never _____ again." (You fill in the blank.) It's possible, for a while anyhow, that you have moments of hope because you think you've prayed hard and God now owes you. But a few more months or perhaps years go by, and all you see is a continuing cycle of stupidity in your kid, and that leaves you depressed and without hope.

Eventually, and out of sheer survival instinct, you decide to "shake off the dust from your feet" and move on. That's also when you tell yourself and others, "That kid will never change." Here you move into accepting the situation because you now know you cannot control or change your child. But keep in mind: Acceptance does not mean you've reached the end of their story or yours. Don't forget that God has a track record of getting through to prodigal kids.[117]

A HEARTBREAKING STORY

If you read my first book, *Epic Grace*, you know I was *that* son. I won't regurgitate all the gory details here, but suffice it to say, I not only broke my wife's heart, but I also crushed my mom's. She once told me

---

117 Luke 15:11–32.

there's nothing more painful than seeing your kids go through hell and not knowing what to do.

A woman in her forties, I'll call her Lindsay, grabbed me after a church service a couple of years ago. I could tell she'd been crying (mascara madness is always a sure sign).

I said, "What's up? Are you okay? How can I pray for you?"

Lindsay let out a deep sigh, covered her face, and began to sob.

I knew her twentysomething daughter was going through a rough time. Lindsay had completed a few prayer request cards at church describing briefly what her daughter Jenni was dealing with. Mostly, it was drug-related, but Jenni was living with a violent man who beat her on a regular basis when he was on meth.

Through her sobs, Lindsay told me Jenni left her boyfriend after his last abusive outrage, but she said, "I'm pretty sure Jenni is living on the streets and probably supporting her drug habit through prostitution."

I hugged Lindsay, told her how sorry I was, and prayed hard for her and her prodigal daughter. After I prayed, she looked me in the eye and said, "I don't know where to turn. Pastor Kurt, what can I do?" The look of hopelessness broke my heart.

Let's take a short look at some of the things I encouraged Lindsay to do.

WHAT TO DO FOR A PRODIGAL

When you have a son or daughter who wanders from God, from you, and from all that is holy, there are some essential things you can work on.

First, ask yourself, "Where am I in the grieving process?" Are you in denial, anger, bargaining, depression, or at some level of acceptance? It's almost impossible to move forward until you realize and admit where you are right now.

The second thing that's imperative for you to do is to take your pain to God. It's normal to vent to your spouse, best friend, maybe your hairdresser, and even your pastor, but don't stop with a human. Take your agony to the Father. He can handle it. Don't hold back. Don't "say a prayer" and gloss over how you feel. Don't think you've got to get all religious with God and say a bunch of hyper-spiritual things to Him. Get real. Don't be disrespectful but do be honest with God. How do you feel? Angry? Sad? Depressed? Discouraged? Tell Him. God is always the best one to cry out to when you're hurting.

Then, after you've gotten honest with yourself and honest with God, offer more counsel to your son or daughter than attempts at control. I know it kills us to watch our teenage or adult kids make the same mistakes we've made, but rather than trying to manage them, provide wise counsel when they ask for it. Most adults don't want or appreciate unsolicited advice, so it's best to wait for them to ask for your guidance. When you give your suggestion, they may or may not listen, but that's up to them. Unfortunately, some lessons seem to be learned only the hard way. And it *is* hard! Hard for them, and hard for you, but an attempt at control is not the solution.

Part of what you're doing is building bridges rather than barriers. Maybe you've noticed when someone hurts us or lets us down, we tend to separate ourselves emotionally and physically from the person who's wounded us. It's in our human nature to protect ourselves by building a barrier around our hearts. When we're hurt, it seems easier to isolate and insulate rather than continue to integrate our lives with our kids. But building and maintaining a bridge is best.

Yes, I know, often a healthy boundary is necessary. There are times when we must create a margin between the other person and us for the safety and health of all. But boundaries and barriers are not the same thing. A boundary is a line put in place as a safety measure. Like the line at a metro rail that warns us, "Be careful. Don't cross this line, or you will be in danger." A barrier is more like the Great Wall of China built to keep people out.

A boundary says, "It's not okay for you to physically, verbally, or emotionally abuse me." (And it's not!) A barrier, however, says, "I have rejected you. Not just what you've done, but who you are, and I want nothing to do with you ever again!" Barriers cut people out of our lives, and that's never the heart of God for anyone.

I see it way too often—a parent (or a child) is extremely wounded, they are deeply disappointed, and then their actions or their words create a Grand Canyon of separation. That is not the heart of God toward us and not the attitude He wants us to have toward our children. In the story of the prodigal son found in Luke 15:18, the son says, "I will set out and go back to my father." This part of the story tells me the father had created and maintained a bridge to his boy. I want to plead with some of you today. Even if your son or daughter has rejected everything you stand for, never reject them. Let them know they will always be precious to you because of who they are, regardless of what they do or don't do. That is the unconditional love and grace God has for us.

Years ago, there was a Motel 6 commercial that said, "We'll leave the lights on for you." My encouragement to you is to keep the light on for your child. Be sure they know there's always a path home for them.

The final thing I'll mention, but it's the most important thing you must do, is to pray. Pray earnestly for your child's repentance and return. I know for a fact God hears the desperate and humble cry of a parent.

When I was far from God in my early twenties, at least two people prayed for me without ceasing: my wife and my momma. And I know I am alive and following Jesus today because of their love and unwavering commitment to pray for me when I was a prodigal son.

Stand in the gap for your child without wavering! Every day and in a thousand ways, bring them to Father God in prayer. Pray the Lord's Prayer: "Father, Your kingdom come, Your will be done in my child's life as it is in heaven!"[118]

---

118 What is commonly referred to as the Lord's Prayer is found in Matthew 6:9–13.

You see, not only does God hear our cries, but there is something about prayer that is good for us too.

- Prayer keeps us focused on the One who can redeem, restore, and renew, and that's the secret to maintaining hope.

- Prayer keeps us humble and desperate for more of God, and more of Him is what we all need.

- Prayer reminds us we are not alone in the spiritual battle for our children!

One of my mentors and heroes in the faith had a daughter who was bitter, angry, and far from God. But I watched and heard that man pray for her many times until she came home, and today that young woman is amazing.

In Luke 18, Jesus told a parable about a persistent widow, and the first verse in that passage tells us the application of the parable. "Then Jesus told his disciples a parable to show them that they should always pray and not give up" (Luke 18:1, NIV). I understand how hard it is to believe your kid will ever change. I know how easy it is to give up. But we must continue to have hope and to pray as if their lives depend on it—because they do!

AFTER THEY COME HOME

When they do come home, please embrace and forgive them without delay. Have you noticed forgiveness is challenging? It's difficult to let the past go. It's hard not to want to make someone pay for all the pain they've caused us.

In the parable of the prodigal son, I used to struggle with relating because of what I often experienced with my dad after I blew it. In the parable, the father celebrated his son's return. He blessed him and threw a party for him.[119] But my dad would say, "I forgive you, but don't you dare do that again! I hope you can see how embarrassed I am. So, the next time will be the last time!"

However, true forgiveness never has a "but" attached to it. We must never say, "I love and forgive you, but . . ." Forgiveness is hard, but it's always the right thing to do, and it must be offered with no strings attached. We forgive because we've been forgiven.

In the parable, when the father saw his son at a distance, he was "filled with love and compassion" and ran to his son! Then, as a demonstrated act of mercy and grace, the father restored and blessed his son without hesitation and without any "I told you so."

Can you imagine how the son must have felt? He had wounded his father, wasted his inheritance, and wandered far. He was filled with shame. But Daddy said, "Let's have a feast and celebrate. For this son of mine was dead and is alive again; he was lost but now is found."

Please don't give up on your kid, and when they do "come home," be watching, be merciful, and be kind.

And be ready to party!

---

119 Luke 15:11–32.

EPIC STEPS

- Create a prayer group with other parents of children who have wandered. Commit to praying together on a regular basis for each prodigal child. Not only will prayer help, but having others in your prayer circle who share a common story will be an additional source of hope for you.

- Begin practicing now the art of forgiveness for your wayward son or daughter. Whether they've come to you yet and asked for it, you can release them from your judgment by choosing to forgive them from your heart today.

SEVENTEEN

HOW TO SURVIVE THE "C" WORD

You cannot change what you are willing to tolerate.
—*Craig Groeschel*

Change. The word excites some of us and terrifies others. Some embrace it; others loathe it. However, like it or not, change is inevitable.

Admittedly, I like change. Before I got old and developed a bad back, I would change the living room furniture on a regular basis. No reason. Just because. Come to think of it, that might be *why* my back is terrible.

For years, I've leased my vehicles because I can get a new and different one every three years. (Sorry, Dave Ramsey, not the wisest use of my resources, I know.) In over forty years of marriage, my wife and I have lived in twenty-two homes. Some would find that reality nightmarish. Not me.

In fact, the only thing I don't change much is what I eat. I'm a pepperoni pizza guy forever. And I do mean forever because I'm sure it's God's choice of pizza too. Steaming hot pepperoni pizza, *without* pineapple, is what I expect to find on the grand banqueting table of heaven.

Yes, I'm ADD and probably ADHD (for real), but nobody ever gets bored hanging out with me—just whiplash. So, if someone is qualified to write about how to thrive in the midst of change, I'm that guy.

YOU'RE OKAY; I'M WEIRD!

I've thought about this a lot. Why do most people struggle so much with change? I've contemplated this because I honestly do want to understand the rest of the world (which includes my wife and most of my children).

First, before I go any further, I'll go on record and say change resistance is normal. The fact that you don't like change doesn't make you weird, boring, or abnormal. You don't need a therapist. There's nothing wrong with you. Really. You're fine.

I'm the strange one.

However, there are two extremes we should avoid.

On the one hand, we shouldn't be addicted to change. Meaning, don't live for the adrenaline rush that comes from something new. I know a guy who is on his fifth wife because he likes the challenge of "breaking in a new one every so often" (his words, not mine). He's selfish and stupid. His change habit has cost him dearly, not to mention it's left a trail of broken hearts. Changing things up just for the sake of change is pointless and frustrating for others. Like any addiction, the first step is to own it. Some of us live in a red zone of constant change, and we need to stop.

I'm the first to admit those who *need* change are often needy and not healthy. For many years now, I've learned to stop and ask myself, "Why are you trying to change _____?" Reflecting on the why question is an exercise that prevents me from changing things just for the sake of change.

On the other hand, the opposite extreme to be avoided is refusing to alter something—or anything—when it truly is time to do so. Being content with pepperoni pizza is one thing; being satisfied with mediocrity is another, and not at all healthy.

My grandmother owned and drove the same white Chevy Impala for most of the twentieth century. In fact, she would drive it cross-country, and it wasn't safe. Hardly anything worked on that beast.

"Grandma, the wipers are worn out, and one of them is broken."

"It's okay. I only need wipers when it's raining."

"Grandma, your car's so out of alignment it shakes when you go above forty."

"Honey, that's why I don't drive in the fast lane on the freeway."

Refusing to change when change is necessary isn't wise; it's foolish. Sorry, Grandma.

WHY SOME STRUGGLE

So, if you're still reading this chapter, congrats! By now, you've had to face some hard-hitting things in this book. Let's finish strong and take a look now at why some people struggle with reasonable and healthy change.

One of the biggest reasons why you struggle with change is due to another "C" word: *comfort*. Some refuse to change because they're comfortable. They've put most everything in their life into cruise mode or on autopilot.

"Sure, my church no longer uses the Bible to teach from, and my pastor is on his third marriage, but it's the church I grew up in."

"Yeah, my spouse is a jerk and a narcissist, but counseling is too expensive and too much work. We just give each other a lot of space, so we're fine."

"I know my bank is lousy and owned by the mafia, but all my bills are set up on autopay."

When you need to change, but you refuse to change because it's too much work or too hard, that's unwise and bordering on laziness. Don't misunderstand me; comfort is not a four-letter word. It's okay to put your feet up and rest. Remember, earlier in this book, I wrote an entire chapter about margin and the need for Sabbath rest (Chapter 9: Turtles Are Not Mutant Ninjas). So, I'm not suggesting being comfortable always equates to being lazy. However, change is often challenging, and I can't ever think of a time in my life when I was both challenged and comfortable at the same time.

When my marriage needs to change and get healthier, that's uncomfortable and takes work.

When I'm trying to lose weight and get in shape, it never starts out as fun (especially 'cause I can't eat unlimited amounts of pepperoni pizza).

When God calls me to a new level of faith and spiritual growth, it's always challenging. Always.

If necessity is the mother of invention, I would like to think that a problematic reality is the mother of alteration. When things get intolerable, you are faced with a choice: deny and die, or change and thrive.

I vote for change.

Jesus once said:

> *There are two paths before you; you may take only one path.* One doorway is narrow. *And one door is wide.* Go through the narrow door. For the wide door leads to a wide path, and the wide path is broad; the wide, broad path is easy, and the wide, broad, easy path has many, many people on it; but the wide, broad, easy, crowded path leads to death. Now then that narrow door leads to a narrow road that in turn leads to life. It is hard to find that road. Not many people manage it.[120]

It sounds a bit like *The Matrix*, doesn't it? There are two pills before you. The red pill or the blue pill. You get to choose; choose wisely.

---

120 Matthew 7:13–14 (The Voice).

Of course, Jesus was referring to those who choose the kingdom of God over hell. However, the principle taught is important to understand. First, we choose. Easy or hard. Good or bad. It's up to us. Second, most prefer the path of least resistance, but that leads to destruction.

Yes, change is tough. Yes, it takes you out of your comfort zone. Yes, it might be easier to take the blue pill and have the story end so you can wake up in your bed and believe whatever you want to believe.

But godly and healthy change is better.

ANOTHER REASON WHY

The desire for comfort is, in my opinion, our greatest foe in the battle with change. Second to that, however, is a four-letter word: *fear*.

Again, I've written about fear in an earlier chapter. I addressed how to face it and why we should bother. Still, anxiety is yet another dragon we must contend with in our make-believe war against change. A thousand "what ifs" plague our mind to the point of crippling us with terror.

"What if I insist we get marriage counseling, and my spouse quits?"

"What if I try to diet, and I fail?"

"What if I say *yes* to God, and it costs me everything?"

Even though we know fear keeps us bound, at least it's a trap we're familiar with and understand.

How sad.

I have a dear friend, Ryan, who stayed at the same miserable job working for a tyrant for years because he was afraid to change companies. He was overworked, underpaid, and unappreciated. For nearly fifteen years, he woke up every morning dreading the workday ahead. Ryan would complain to me on a regular basis, "I hate my job. I hate my boss. I think I work in hell."

One day, after countless times of grumbling to me about his lousy job over lunch, I finally said, "Dude, for heaven's sake, just quit! I'm exhausted listening to your bellyaching all the time. Your wife must be going crazy! You're a talented guy with a job skill that's in demand. Why are you putting up with this day after day and year after year?" (Tenderness as a pastor isn't something I'm known for.)

Ryan admitted, "I am afraid."

"I know, my friend, I know, but misery is worse than fear."

It was a bit like the heavens parted for him at that moment. He said, "You're right! I'd rather be poor and happy than employed and cranky!"

He quit.

That day.

Two days later, Ryan got the job of his dreams making almost twice as much money.

Sure, I understand. Not all stories have happy endings. I get it. Sometimes we embrace change, and things go sideways. I know. But unrealistic fears lead to unreasonable acceptance of things that must change.

Face your fear. Admit it for what it is: a lack of faith in the goodness of God. Then embrace change as a friend rather than an enemy.

YEAH, BUT . . .

About now you might be thinking, *I hear what you're saying, Bubna, but as you said, change doesn't always end with me in a happy place. What then?*

What I'm going to write next is difficult to read. You might want to take a deep breath or at least grab some comfort food before you read on.

Most change is meant to mold us.

I wish I could tell you all change, though hard, will make you happy eventually, but it may not. The commitment and promise from

God is to perfect and mature us.[121] The apostle Paul was confident God "who began a good work in you will carry it on to completion," but there's never any promise of an easy life.[122]

Here's the thing: The dross and junk in most of us only get removed as the heat gets turned up in our lives. The parts of us that are not like Jesus tend to get removed through radical surgery, and not through a little liposuction here and there.

You and I get shaped, carved, and eventually molded into the image of Christ through change we'd rather not go through, thank-you-very-much.

I get cancer, and I learn to eat better.

I get hurt, and I learn to love better.

I get surprised, and I learn to trust better.

I get mad, irritated, upset, and frustrated with family, friends, my spouse (or all of the above), and I learn to forgive.

The painful stuff is used by God to make me more like Jesus and a better me. As my friend Dr. Jeff Kennedy says, "The you God builds in the storm is a better you." In other words, some things happen best in the dark, and often you and I grow best when all hell is breaking loose. Why? Because that's where we discover that the gates of hell cannot prevail against the work of God in our lives.

Here's the bad news/good news.

Bad news: Life is hard. Change is tough. You are a work in progress, and progress is often painful.

Good news: God's still working on you, and change is good for you even when it's hard.

So don't fight change, and guard your heart through the process so you become better rather than bitter.

Change is not your enemy.

Really.

You'll be okay.

---

121 Ephesians 4:15.

122 Philippians 1:6.

Because God promises to mold you into the person you truly do want to be, and that always involves change.[123]

A lot of change.

---

123 Philippians 1:6.

EPIC STEPS

- Do you generally embrace change or resist it? Take a moment and consider why.

- What was the last major change you made in your life? Was it for a good reason or not? List the results—good or bad—that came about because of this change. How did God use this situation to mold you into the image of His Son?

- Make a short list of some things that probably should change in your life. What will it take for you to get out of your comfort zone and move forward?

- Go order a pepperoni pizza (without pineapple)!

THE LONG JOURNEY TO HOPE

In the struggle between the stone and water, in time, the water wins.
—Japanese Proverb

Throughout this book, I've done my best to encourage you. Hope is always possible. Perhaps not easy, but not beyond your reach. You truly can do more than just survive in life's storms; you can thrive in the midst of your darkest night. No matter what you feel like or see around you, God is the "Father of compassion and the God of all comfort."[124] He will never give up on you, so hope is yours for the taking.

A few years ago, a young man named Toby came to me extremely discouraged. He was unhappy with his wife and disheartened by his lack of spiritual growth. And the icing on the cake was he had some horrible habits.

Toby said, "It's hopeless. My marriage will never change, and I will never change."

Here's what I told him, and it's true for *all* of us.

---

124 2 Corinthians 1:3 (NIV).

It takes three things to experience lasting change: 1) a desire; 2) a choice; and 3) an encounter with God and the power of His Spirit.

No one changes until they *want* to change, and that has a lot to do with our attitude and desire.

No one changes until they *elect* to change, and that has a lot to do with our decisions and choices.

No one changes, truly changes at a heart and soul level, until they *cry out to God*.

We humans have a way of doing what we want to do when we want it badly enough. However, nothing happens until we make a choice—often a daily choice—to do what must be done. And the key to consistent success is empowerment by the Holy Spirit; He helps us to do what we know we can't do on our own.

Whatever your struggle, whatever your battle, whatever you're carrying from your past, dealing with in your present, or might face in your future, remember that nothing is too hard for God.[125] Absolutely nothing. And always remember this: Uncommon hope comes from knowing your pain is never wasted when God is in the mix.

Near the end of Paul's letter to the church in Rome, he wrote to Christians who were struggling, "May the God of hope fill you with all joy and peace as you trust in him, so that you may overflow with hope by the power of the Holy Spirit."[126]

That, my friend, is my desire for you. As you trust in Him, you can and will experience a peace that seems ludicrous to a watching world. And the more you trust God, the more the Lord's hope will overflow through you to others—not by your power, but by His.

Jesus loves you more than His own life and more than you can imagine.

So, let hope rise in you as you fix your eyes on Him so you can live the epic life He has planned for you.

It won't always be easy.

But it will always be worth it.

---

125 Jeremiah 32:26; Matthew 19:26.

126 Romans 15:13 (NIV).

LET ME PRAY FOR YOU

Jesus, we are broken, desperate, often confused, and hopeless without you. Thank you for being so understanding, patient, and kind with cracked jars of clay. Just as you pressed through your darkest moment on the cross, help us to stay the course too. Help us remain fixed on you. Help us when we are helpless and afraid. God of all comfort, please wrap your arms around our hearts and hold us tight. We need you. Always have. Always will. Amen.

ACKNOWLEDGMENTS

Everyone needs a tribe of hope around them that will stand by their side no matter what may come. I am blessed to have the support of so many incredible people.

- My wife who has partnered with me in life and ministry for almost forty-five years.

- The staff at Eastpoint Church who consistently put up with my stories and often become the source of some good ones.

- The people of Eastpoint Church who sometimes believe in me more than I believe in myself.

- Jessica Harris, Lindsay Branting, and Karen Reinhart who faithfully provided early editing support.

- Melinda Martin who designed an awesome cover and handled the formatting of this book.

- Shayla Raquel who is, hands down, the best editor I've ever worked with in my life.

KURT BUBNA

K URT BUBNA has been in pastoral ministry since 1976 and now serves as the founding and senior pastor of Eastpoint Church in Spokane Valley, Washington.

He has worked extensively as a speaker, international trainer, and short-term missionary in Botswana, Great Britain, Mexico, Guatemala, Nepal, India, and Sri Lanka.

Additionally, Kurt is a certified church consultant through Thom Rainer's Church Consultant University, and for many years, he has trained and coached numerous pastors throughout the United States and Africa.

For more information on his speaking availability and engagements, please see KurtBubna.com. For information about his pastoral coaching or church consulting company, please visit ReviveCoachingGroup.com.

CONNECT WITH THE AUTHOR

Website	kurtbubna.com	**Twitter**	Twitter.com/kurtbubna
Coaching	revivecoachinggroup.com	**Instagram**	Instagram.com/kurtbubna
Facebook	Facebook.com/kurtbubna	**LinkedIn**	Linkedin.com/in/ kurt-bubna-64083229

LEAVE A REVIEW

If you enjoyed this book, will you please consider writing a review on Amazon and Goodreads?